Information Technology and Economic Growth

Information Technology and Economic Growth

Study of Leading States in India

R.G. DESAI

RAWAT PUBLICATIONS

Jaipur • New Delhi • Bangalore • Mumbai

ISBN 81-7033-953-7

Published by
Prem Rawat for *Rawat Publications*
Satyam Apts., Sector 3, Jawahar Nagar, Jaipur 302 004 (India)
Phone: 0141 265 1748 / 7006 Fax: 0141 265 1748
E-mail: info@rawatbooks.com
Website: www.rawatbooks.com

Delhi Office
4858/24, Ansari Road, Daryaganj, New Delhi 110 002
Phone: 011-23263290

Also at Bangalore and Mumbai

Typeset by Rawat Computers, Jaipur
Printed at Chaman Enterprises, New Delhi

Contents

Acknowledgements

This manuscript is the outcome of my work as visiting Fellow at Institute for Social and Economic Change (ISEC), Nagarabhavi, Bangalore, during 2003. I am ever grateful to *K.K. Birla Foundation, New Delhi* for awarding me one year Fellowship to complete the project on *Economics of Information Technology: A Study of Leading States in India.* My thanks are due to our vice-chancellor, M.S. Thimmappa, and R. Veerachamy, Chairman, Dept. of Economics, Bangalore University, for their help in sanction of sabbatical leave to complete this fellowship programme at ISEC.

I am also grateful to the chairman of ISEC, T.R. Satishchandran, former director, Govinda Rao and present director of ISEC, Gopal Kadekodi for grant of academic affiliation and for providing working space, computer, Internet and library facilities without which my work could not have been moved at this speed.

I thank heartily all the faculty in ISEC, for their constant support, cooperation and encouragement received from time to time; specially I thank M.R. Narayana, R.S. Deshpande, Seetharamu, S.N. Sangita, K.N. Ninan, M. Mahadeva, and others in the Institute. My thanks are due to several persons in library and computer sections. Krishnachandra, Satish Kamat and their team were very helpful to me in browsing through several websites.

My respectful thanks are due to Abdul Aziz, retired professor of ISEC and former member of State Finance Commission, Government of Karnataka for his valuable comments on the earlier version of this volume; however usual disclaimers apply. My thanks are due to D.S. Deepa, project assistant for her constant help and assistance in putting together the entire manuscript and making it ready for publication. Finally, I thank profusely Pranit Rawat of Rawat Publications for the neat publication of the book.

R.G. Desai

Abbreviations

AICTE	All India Council for Technical Education
APDMS	Andhra Pradesh Development Monitor System
APIIC	Andhra Pradesh Industry Infrastructure Corporation
APSWAN	Andhra Pradesh State Wide Area Network
BPO	Business Process Outsourcing
CAG	Comptroller and Auditor General
CAGR	Cumulative Annual Growth Rate
CARD	Computer Aided Registration Department
C-DAC	Center for Developing Advanced Computing
CEO	Chief Executive Officer
CIF	Common Intermediate Format
CLI	Common Language Interface/ Command Line Interface
CMM	Capability Maturity Model
CST	Central Sale Tax
DTA	Domestic Tariff Area
DoT	Department of Telecom
DRDA	District Rural Development Authority
ECP	Extended Capabilities Port
EOU	Export Oriented Unit
EPZ	Export Processing Zone
ERP	Enterprise Resource Planning

EHTP	Electronic Hardware Technology Park
ESOP	Employee Stock Option Plan
ESOS	Employee Stock Option Scheme
FAST	Fully Automated Services of Transport
FDI	Foreign Direct Investment
FMCG	Fast Moving Consuming Goods
gbps	Giga Byte Per Second
GDP	Gross Domestic Product
GIS	Geographical Information System
G2C	Government to Citizen
ICT	Information and Communication Technology
IDC	International Data Corporation
ILDO	International Long Distance Operators
IP	Internet Protocol
IPR	Intellectual Property Rights
ISD	International Subscriber's Dialing
IT	Information Technology
ITeS	Information Technology Enabled Service
ISP	Internet Service Provider
K-BITS	Karnataka-Biotechnology and Information Technology Services
kbps	Kilo Byte Per Second
KEONICS	Karnataka State Electronic's Development Corporation Limited
KSSIDC	Karnataka State Small Industry Development Corporation
KIADB	Karnataka Industrial Area Development Board
MCA	Master of Computer Application
mbps	Mega Byte Per Second
MIN	Multiple Identity Number
MIS	Management Information System
MNC	Multi-National Corporation

MOU	Memorandum of Understanding
MPCB	Maharashtra Pollution Control Board
MTNL	Mahanagar Telephone Nigam Limited
NASSCOM	National Association of Software and Service Companies
NCAER	National Council for Applied Economic Research
NCR	National Capital Region
NFEE	Net Foreign Exchange Earning
NIC	National Informatics Centre
NOC	No Objection Certificate
RAS	Remote Access Server
RTC	Record of Rights, Tenancy and Crops
SARI	Sustainable Access in Rural India
SCM	Supply Chain Management
SDP	State Domestic Product
SDSL	Series of Digital Subscriber Lines
SET	Secure Electronic Transaction
SEZ	Special Economic Zone
SKIMS	Secretarial Knowledge and Information System
SME	Small and Medium Enterprise
STPI	Software Technology Park of India
STP	Software Technology Park
STD	Subscriber Trunk Dialing
SSID	Service Set Identifier
tbps	Tera Byte Per Second
UPS	Uninterrupted Power Supply
URL	Universal Resource Locator
vBNS	very high-speed Backbone Network Service
VCC	Venture Capital Company
VCF	Venture Capital Fund
VCU	Venture Capital Undertaking
VSAT	Very Small Aperture Terminal

VSNL	Videsh Sanchar Nigam Limited
VoIP	Voice over Internet Protocol
VPN	Virtual Private Network
WiLL	Wireless-in Local Loop
WWV	Warana Wired Village project
xDSL	Series of Digital Subscriber Lines

List of Tables

List of Figures and Charts

Figures

Charts

Introduction

India's achievement in information technology at present has enviable track record. What started off as a pure resource pool for fulfilling programming demands of other countries, has now changed substantially in scope. Over the years, the term 'information technology' has become more widespread and now encompasses several sectors of the economy and has created several opportunities. Yet, there are some common threads, lessons and success factors we have identified from the past success in pure software development. The present work gives an analysis of the state of information technology in India with special emphasis on the exponential growth of information technology industry in selected leading states.

The principal objective of the study is to assess the role of information technology in economic development in general and Indian economy in particular. While dealing with the former, the studies relating to the experiences of the developed countries have been heavily borrowed and quoted. But when it comes to Indian information technology, the role of software technology parks and proactive policy of governments (both centre and state government) are widely discussed. Further, to identify the success of e-governance, some successful information technology projects in selected states have been analyzed dispassionately in this study.

Analytically, the contribution of information technology to an economy could be viewed at two different but interrelated levels: on account of information technology growth and on account of information technology diffusion. The former refers to the contribution in output, employment, export earning, etc., on account of the production of information technology related goods and services which are confined to just one segment of the economy and the latter refers to information technology induced development through enhanced productivity competitiveness, growth and human welfare on account of the use of this technology by the different sectors of the economy and society. The nature of benefits that an economy derives from the information technology sector depends *inter alia*, on the character of the information technology sector. This is because in analyzing the process of diffusion one has to take into account both the forces of demand and supply.

India's attempt has been mainly to profit from information technology growth, through a series of institutional innovations and export-oriented policy measures. Hence, the often claimed achievements with respect to Indian information technology have not been in terms of harnessing the new technology for enhanced efficiency and productivity growth; instead it is in terms of export earning for the economy. Indeed, the export performance, not only in terms of the magnitude of observed growth rates but also in terms of its stability, has been unique when compared to any other products in our export basket. Therefore, general objective of this study is to assess the information technology scenario in India and the specific objectives are as follows:

- To review studies relating to investment in information technology and productivity at cross-countries level.
- To assess the growth of information technology sector in the country since 1991 and to know the interrelations between hardware, software and information technology enabled services with special reference to economic

variables such as gross output and earnings, employment, etc., in the country.
- To study the role of Software Technology Parks in promoting information technology sector.
- To examine the taxes, incentives and regulations in promoting the information technology sector both at the Centre and in states.
- To analyse the causes and consequences for exponential growth of information technology in certain states and its slow diffusion to other parts of the region.
- To know the impact of information technology on social sector through e-governance projects in leading states.
- To identify the crucial issues and challenges faced by information technology sector in general, and suggest policy implications.

While substantial work has been done on information technology and productivity (usually known as 'productivity paradox') across the world, the area of research in India appears to be confined to the growth of information technology sector at the national level, based on the data from NASSCOM and *Dataquest*.

Further, no study has been attempted to analyse the intricacies and impact of information technology at sub-national or regional level. The need of such study arises in view of widening digital divide within the economy and regional information technology disparities among the states of Indian economy.

In studying the comparative advantages of certain states, researchable questions were:

- Do investment in information technology sector propelled as an engine of growth in the state's economy during liberalization period?
- Whether information technology sector development is based on comparative advantage of certain states?
- What is the role of software technology parks in promoting information technology in the country?

- Whether diffusion of information technology to other sectors/states has succeeded?
- Have declining computer prices generated sizeable benefits to different sector through favourable state policies?
- Has public-private partnership in e-governance succeeded or not?

The scope of the study covers information technology development in the country since 1991 and specifically inquired about four aspects:

- Growth of information technology gross output and revenue earnings;
- Employment generation and its nature;
- Interrelations between hardware, software and information technology enabled services, and
- E-governance in leading states of India.

The first two objectives of the present study are based on the data collected from NASSCOM. Time series data pertaining software exports, bandwidth availability, number of units registered, number of software technology parks and their contribution are collected from the website: indiastat.com and compared across the states. As far as other objectives are concerned (role of information technology in administration, rural economy and e-governance), the data from the respective state's websites as well as field data from 100 sample farmers in four divisions of Karnataka for e-governance project on 'Bhoomi' is collected and assessed the welfare gain and loss. Forerunner states such as Karnataka, Andhra Pradesh, Maharashtra and Tamil Nadu are chosen based on the successful experiments of their information technology e-governance projects. However, the information technology policy impact is assessed based on the benefits accrued to the public.

Chapter 1 deals with theoretical and conceptual issues in general. Several studies have been discussed. The studies of Negroponte (1995), Kraemer and Dedrick (1994), Schware (1992) and Romer (1993) have been widely used. The fundamental idea is to bring out the sharp difference between the tangible goods and intangible goods in the economic system. Economic value is embedded more and more in tangible goods than in physical form. The typical example is the Demat scheme of Indian stock market. Most of the companies in India have now made it compulsory to keep the share certificates not in physical form but in Demat form called 'E-Share'. This process of dematerialization derives from the increasing output share of all services in general and from growing importance of information technology in particular.

The experiences of other countries has shown that slow diffusion of information technology is one of the possible explanations for negative correlation between information technology investment and economy-wide productivity.

According to Solow (1987), "you can see the computer age everywhere but not in the productivity statistics". This came to be popularly known as 'productivity paradox'. However, as the information technology has grown over decades, this negative correlation is replaced by positive correlation. This has been revealed not only at cross-country level studies but also at economy level and even at the firm's level studies. Thus, it is now remarked that "paradox is lost". Of course, these country level studies and micro-level studies may pertain to highly potential countries and potential firms but not all. Hence, still, there is a big challenge to prove positive productivity relation with investment. However, if there is a proactive and effective policies of the countries in close consultation with the private sector and academic institutions and if the efforts of related government agencies can be coordinated, the results can be a rapid diffusion of the technology with broad benefits for the country.

Chapter 2 deals with actual experience of the information technology revolution in India. Here, the role of NASSCOM as a guiding force of the Indian information technology sector is highlighted.

The success of information technology albeit from a low base to dynamism has proved the often quoted Moore's Law "output that entered commercial production every 18-24 months incorporate twice the number". For instance, over the 12 years period 1990-91 to 2001-02, the annual compound rate of growth of information technology output in India was 37.4 per cent, i.e., output was doubling every 2.2 years. Further, the gross earnings from the software exports as well as the generation of employment and its nature are widely discussed.

However, structure of industry is undergoing a formidable change, viz.,

(1) During 1990s contribution of domestic segment was 80 per cent of total information technology industry's output while export segment was 20 per cent. But, by 2000-01, export segment has increased to 60 per cent and domestic segment to 40 per cent.
(2) In the early years of its development the success of information technology was onsite, later it has changed to offshore. Now, it is the Business Process Outsourcing (BPO) and Information Technology Enabled Services (ITeS).
(3) Similarly, in the early 1990s, the information technology giants like Infosys, Wipro, Tata Consultancy Services (TCS) have captured the attention of both the government as well as bureaucrats. Now, attention is towards SMEs (small and medium enterprises) whose contribution has increased much in the last year.

In Chapter 3, the role of software technology parks (STPs) has been highlighted. Software technology park scheme is for the development of export of software on the lines of special economic zones or 100 per cent export-oriented units. Since their inception, the contribution of software technology parks to the total information technology exports is enormous.

Software technology parks act as a catalyst in boosting the exports, by providing not only concession incubation centres and government tax benefits, but also free involvement with clients and their interest – that is the speciality of the this new agent. The role of software technology park is now such that nearly 80 per cent of the total information technology exports are only from the firms registered through software technology park in different parts of the country. However, there is lot of variation across the states and highly tilted towards the southern states of Karnataka, Maharashtra, Tamil Nadu and Andhra Pradesh.

Chapter 4 discusses tax exemptions, concessions, support services, relaxation, laws and regulations pertaining to information technology sector. In this chapter, exemption from custom duties, income tax provisions, special incentives of the state government have been discussed. The concessions and rebate varied from state to state. For instance, in Karnataka, 15 per cent of cost of land is given as rebate after commissioning the information technology unit. Whereas in Andhra Pradesh, rebate is linked to the job creation and restricted to Rs. 20,000 per job created in each unit. While Tamil Nadu gives investment subsidy to information technology units on basis of 20 per cent of the capital investment, the Maharashtra government directed all municipal corporations to exempt from levy of octroi or tax on entry of imported capital and raw materials for IT and ITeS units. In this section, there is also discussion on India's first cyber law and regulatory norms of the Indian cyber space. It is followed by comments and conclusion.

Chapter 5 contains the heart of the study and analysis surrounds the core issues raised in the research proposal. The regional growth experience of the 1990s suggests that the states pursuing reforms seemed to have experienced higher growth rates than other states.

This is strikingly evident in terms of number of factories, fixed capital investment, employment and the gross value added during 1990-91 to 2000-01. In terms of employment, Tamil Nadu, Andhra Pradesh, Karnataka and Maharashtra emerged more prominent. In terms of development and penetration of information technology, the same four states have been regarded as leaders.

This fact is proved in this work by supporting the empirical data collected mostly from the several websites in the Internet as well as personal visits to several software technology parks. Leading role of the three southern states and Maharashtra is considered on the basis four criteria, viz., supply of information technology skilled workers, infrastructure, specially bandwidth, policy environment of the state government and successful e-governance projects.

Chapter 6 deals with e-governance and role of information technology in administration. In the beginning, the difference is made out clearly between e-governance and e-government. Five success e-governance projects have been widely discussed, one each from the state of Karnataka, Andhra Pradesh, Madhya Pradesh, Maharashtra and Tamil Nadu. The Bhoomi project of Karnataka, Gyandoot project of Madhya Pradesh, Warana Wired Village project of Maharashtra and Sustainable Access in Rural India project of Tamil Nadu have tremendous impact on the rural folk, whereas the e-Seva project of Andhra Pradesh has much impact on the urban people. This chapter kindles the hopes of policy makers in other states to follow suit, as it will not only try to bridge the digital divide but will also influence the voting pattern of rural folks.

Chapter 7 tackles issues and challenges faced by the information technology sector. Among several issues, issue of bandwidth and connectivity problems are highlighted. The fast growth of information technology sector also created labour related issues.

Among them, the problem of labour attrition, the flexible nature of the working conditions, uncertainty looming over the large part of labour force are discussed. Regarding the challenges, competition from China may be a big threat to the information technology sector in India. Challenges relating to hardware sector still looms large. At the end, suggestions are offered for policy implications.

Conclusion

There is a constant shift taking place in the structure of information technology in India. In the beginning, it was heavily concentrated on programming to foreign clients, next exports of software and services dominated. The emphasis is now on business process outsourcing and IT-enabled services. However, a shift from few big companies dominating in the field (as oligopolists) to more number of small and medium enterprises is a welcome trend. In each chapter there is lesson to the policy makers to note.

(1) The most effective policy for country is to promote information technology use and production close to use as well as that build capabilities.

(2) Without policy intervention and establishment of software technology parks at remote areas, information technology will intensify social divisions rather than close them. Easy access to information technology enable people to improve their standard of living and this could be made possible by effective private-public partnership.

(3) The fast growth of information technology sector is partly due to exemption from taxes, concessions and rebate on land acquisition, relaxations in Acts as well as support service rendered by the state governments. There is a lesson to other non-leading states to follow the suit.

(4) The causes and consequences of information technology revolution concentrated in select leading states in India brings to the forefront that investment in infrastructure, physical, capital and education is the key to economic development. This is of course an old policy prescription in the economics of development. What is new in the analyses is the view that information technology content of these investments should be high.

(5) Information technology gives hopes to other states, regarded as 'aspiring' and 'laggards' to look forward and understand the role of software technology parks as a

catalyst agent and consider its success in certain states due to highly skilled cheap labours. There is a lesson to those states that no single state can ignore any longer the needs to invest in these technologies if it wants to improve the standard of living of its citizens.

(6) The e-governance projects exhibit a clear message that "nothing succeeds like success". It contains some success stories. Behind every success, there is an involvement of committed people from private, public and even local levels. Unless such tribe is increasing in number the success of information technology will be just like another revolution in the Indian economy.

(7) Information technology sector like any other sector has created several problems and issues. Among them, labour related issues, bandwidth and connectivity problems are more burning. Here, all states will have to take the measures for smooth resolving the issues and implementation of the recommendations made in this study will go a long way in boosting equitable growth in the information technology sector.

It is hoped that this study undertaken for K.K. Birla Foundation, New Delhi will provide useful policy inputs for the other state governments, which are lagging behind in the information technology adoption. We also hoped that implementations of the recommendations made in the study will contribute to policy reform to ensure greater productivity and employment and will also close the digital divide.

1

Role of Information Technology in Economic Development

The truly revolutionary aspect of modern information technology is believed to be the possibility it offers to unbundled information from its physical carrier. This means that the economics of information can be separated from the economics of things. The 'information superhighway' is, as Negroponte (1995) has defined it, "about the global movement of weightless bits at the speed of light". Quah (2001) argues that it is this increasing weightlessness or dematerialization of production that is characteristic of modern economies. By this he means that an increasingly greater fraction of gross domestic product comes to reside in economic goods with little or no physical manifestation. Economic value is embedded more and more in intangible goods than in physical objects. This process of dematerialization derives from the increasing output share of all services in general and from the growing importance of information technology in particular.

The existing explanations for the persistent poverty of developing nations can be summarized into the two extreme views (Romer, 1993). The first view is based on an 'object gap'. A country is poor because it lacks objects, which are valuable in production. These include raw materials, physical capital in the form of engines, factories, and roads, as well as human capital in the form of educated labour. The second view is based on an 'ideas gap'. A country is poor because it does not have access to the ideas that are used in industrial nations to generate economic value. Ideas are the instructions that are needed to combine physical resources to produce economically valuable commodities. These explanations are not necessarily mutually exclusive because a nation can suffer from both gaps at the same time.

Ideas are different from objects in the sense that they have no opportunity costs. Invention, innovation, discovery and technological change are all activities that increase the stock of intangible knowledge or ideas. Unlike physical goods, an idea is something that you can give to someone else and yet still retain it for your own use. The Pythagoras theorem, a computer software code or a blueprint for manufacturing are examples. Once invented, they can be copied and transferred at negligible cost. Ideas are in fact infinitely expansible (or non-rival), in the sense that their use by one person or by one country does not prevent others from using them. This property makes them fundamentally different from physical commodities. Information may be appropriable in the sense that others may have high obstacles of obtaining it, but it typically entails a non-rival use.

Ideas are indeed dematerialized and weightless. Economists and policy makers alike have, however, known their importance for economic growth and development, invention, and patents. As Quah (2001) explains, to understand the essential aspects of the information technology, or of information society at large, it is helpful to make a distinction between those ideas which have economic value in their physical manifestation only and those ideas which retain their value independent of the physical medium containing them. The printing press, the spinning jenny, the steam engine and the railway are examples of the first group of commodities. They all have a very high idea content, and each one of them has certainly made a significant contribution to technological progress and economic development. However, they would have been worthless if the underlying ideas had never taken these specific physical forms.

The second, weightless group of commodities includes, for example, computer software, telecommunications, semiconductors, biological algorithms, financial services, electronic databases and libraries, media entertainment and Internet delivery of goods and services. All these commodities can be expressed in binary bits of logic. Their economic value is independent from their physical carriers. The thesis of dematerialization is that economic value will increasingly be created by producing and distributing bits of logic rather than atoms of physical material.

While computers and information technology form a large part of this activity, the digitalization of production and consumption means that an increasing number of products and services become idea-like goods or knowledge products. These products are so called because their physical properties resemble those of knowledge, not necessarily because they are knowledge and science intensive in production. In fact, as Quah (2001) explains, an economy can be knowledge intensive because of the quantity of knowledge products consumed.

The policy implications of the idea and object gap views of economic development are quite different. The object gap view emphasizes the role of saving and investment in both physical capital and education. The ideas gap explanation highlights the need for the transfer of technology from the developed countries to the developing ones. It directs attention to the patterns of interaction and communication between a developing country and the rest of the world. Extending the concept of the idea gap to cover the gap in idea-like or knowledge goods, attention is also drawn to the role of demand in generating such goods and, consequently, economic growth and technological development. As will be explained below, modern information technology reduces the 'distance' between producers and consumers of knowledge products, making the pattern of demand an influential factor of economic growth. Thus, it is called death of a distance. The question about intellectual property rights to such products also arises naturally in this context. Knowledge goods are not typically made excludable by patents but, like literary works, they are protected by copyright.

Rebelo surveys models which make technological progress endogenous by allowing firms to undertake investment aimed either at producing new goods or at developing new production methods. These theories assume that there are skilled workers who as researchers, scientists or inventors generate ideas and new knowledge. The greater the number of such producers of knowledge, the faster economy grows. Skilled workers, however, face competing uses for their time and expertise. They can decide to work in other professions: to become, for example, mangers, production workers or lawyers. In equilibrium, returns equalize across different activities for skilled workers, thereby determining the growth rate of the economy.

As Quah (2001) points out, these growth models assume the existence of a system of intellectual property rights. Upon obtaining a useful idea, the researcher obtains a patent for it, and sells the patent to a firm producing intermediate goods. This firm then rents the intermediate goods built around the original idea to a monopolistically competitive manufacturing firm which produces final consumption products by combining the intermediate goods with labour and skilled managerial input.

Rebelo demonstrates that economic growth depends positively on the size of the market in these models. This implication is empirically counter-factual since there is no relation between population size and rates of growth in cross-country data. These models may, however, be relevant for only a handful of advanced economies that undertake significant R&D investments and that, consequently, are on the frontier of technological development. Since these economies export their products, the relevant size of the market is the whole world.

For most economies around the world the issue is not whether to devote resources to innovation, but whether to adopt technologies that have been developed by others. The review of the models of technology adoption shows that decreases in the price of new capital goods tend to increase economic growth. But if it takes time and resources to operate a new technology, a major technological revolution, such as the information technology revolution, may be associated with a prolonged decline in productivity as shown, for example, by David (2000), and Greenwood and Yorukoglu (1997). This learning period is also characterized by increasing wage inequality since skilled labour has an advantage at learning and since the advance in technology is associated with an increase in the demand for skills needed to implement it. The slow diffusion of information technology is one of the possible hypotheses explaining the observed negative correlation between information technology investment and economy wide productivity in the United States (a review by Kraemer and Dedrick-1994).

This 'productivity paradox' of information technology is often summarized by referring to Solow's (1987) much quoted sentence "you can see the computer age everywhere but in the productivity statistics".

Mohnen takes up the issue of the international diffusion of technology. The information technology sector is one of the leading sectors in terms of R&D effort. In the leading industrial countries, R&D in computer and office equipment, communications equipment, and electronic equipment accounts for one third to one sixth of total business R&D expenditures. The returns from research in information technologies should be widespread given their pervasive use. Moreover, information technology plays a leading role in knowledge creation, codification, and transmission. Mohnen summarizes the empirical findings on international R&D spillovers with a particular attention devoted to information technology and to spillovers from industrial to developing countries.

The review demonstrates that international R&D spillovers are significant whether in terms of social rates of return, elasticities of TFP (total factor productivity) growth or growth contributions. Some calculations indicate that in 1990 the R&D spillover-effects from industrial countries have increased output in developing countries by about 21 billion US dollars, compared to the official development aid of about 50 billion. Other calculations show that, if all industrial countries raise their R&D spending by half a per cent of GDP, output increases by 14 per cent in the long run in all developing countries. With the increase in trade, economic integration, the spread of multinationals, the globalization of the economy and the development of information technology we expect an ever increasing importance of technology sourcing.

Few studies have examined the role of information technology as spillover emitters and as spillover transmitters, but they give a lot of credit to information technology in embodying new technology. As information technology becomes widespread, as more and more production and commerce takes place electronically, it becomes essential for developing countries to assimilate the electronic technologies required to participate in the global innovation network.

Quah (2001) explores the importance of the demand side for technological change and economic growth, with special reference to the development of information technology. Knowledge and technology have long been recognized to be important in economic growth, as Revelo's survey demonstrates. But in the received growth theory, consumers are assumed to come into contact with knowledge only through physical goods embodying the new technology. They are distant from the producers of knowledge and need not even be aware of the properties of knowledge as a product, like infinite expansibility.

Quah's key idea is that modern technologies associated with knowledge products reduce the distance between consumers on the one hand and knowledge-based production on the other. As a result, demand-side factors such as consumer attitudes on sophisticated goods, training, education and skills for consumption (rather than production) importantly influence patterns of technological development, and therefore economic growth and development more generally. The failure of the industrial revolution to occur in the technologically advanced China of the 14th century is given as an example of how a change in consumer attitudes to sophisticated technology can result in economic growth slowing down or even failing to occur. The supply of technology was present there, but the changing pattern of demand for technology by the state in China led to technology first growing, then languishing and finally regressing.

The analysis of the distance between consumers and knowledge-based production is based on the observation that knowledge products, like computer software, are not typically made excludable by patents, but they are copyrighted like literary works. Copyright is not an intellectual property right allowing excludability and monopolistic production and preventing other users from copying the product. In fact, knowledge products are easily copied even under copyright law. The cost to a consumer of using a specific knowledge product comes not only from the norms, conventions and subtleties involved in using the product. These learning costs explain why the weak protection offered by copyright law can be sustained.

Quah (2001) argues that, given the infinite expansibility of knowledge products, the supply of information technology is not a factor that restrains economic growth and development. How growth will unfold depends on consumer attitudes to sophisticated goods, on the intellectual property regime that fosters development of technology and on the equilibrium reactions of the supply side.

The model he presents can produce a range of equilibria, depending on the distribution of the hedonic cost of consumption of knowledge goods. In some equilibria, the knowledge-product industry grows rapidly, whereas in other it languishes. Some equilibria may even display leapfrogging phenomena: consumers (or economies) having lowest opportunity costs of using sophisticated products can end up becoming users of high-quality knowledge products.

The study has two important policy implications. First, it shows that training and education are important, not just in providing skills for work and production, but in providing a sufficiently strong demand base. Besides having access to the new technology, it is important that people participate in the information economy. This can be achieved through government policies which reduce the hedonic costs of using them. Unless a demand side can be cultivated that appreciates and exploits sophisticated and advancing technology, economic growth can slow or, ultimately, collapse. Government policies that strongly curtail private use of new technologies can have adverse long-run consequences on economic growth.

Virtuous Circle between Information Technology Investment and Economic Factors

We use the conceptual model developed in Kraemer and Dedrick (1994) as a framework for new studies that have been undertaken with much larger databases. The framework posits a virtuous circle between information technology investments and economic factors. The first half of the virtuous circle is illustrated by the economic factors that drive information technology investments: national wealth, wage rates, its infrastructure and the price/performance of information technology products.

Growing national wealth provides the resources for investments in information technology, both by businesses and by households. Increases in wages provide a greater incentive for organizations (firms, governments) to invest in information technology, either to replace workers or to improve the productivity of workers.

The presence of a high quality information infrastructure, in the form of communications networks and skilled human resources, increases the potential value of information technology investments and thus promotes such investments. Finally, the ongoing improvements in information technology price/performance encourages continued investment to take advantage of ever greater capabilities of the technology at lower prices.

The curved lines in Figure 1.1 illustrate the other half of the virtuous circle, showing how information technology investments can lead to economic growth. Increased labour productivity means an economy can support higher wages, which lead to increased personal income and consumption. Increased capital productivity supports higher returns on investments by organizations, and indirectly by individual investors (for example, stockholders). Thus, a given level of capital investment can result in higher returns in the form of

Figure 1.1

Virtuous Circle between IT Investment and Economic Factors

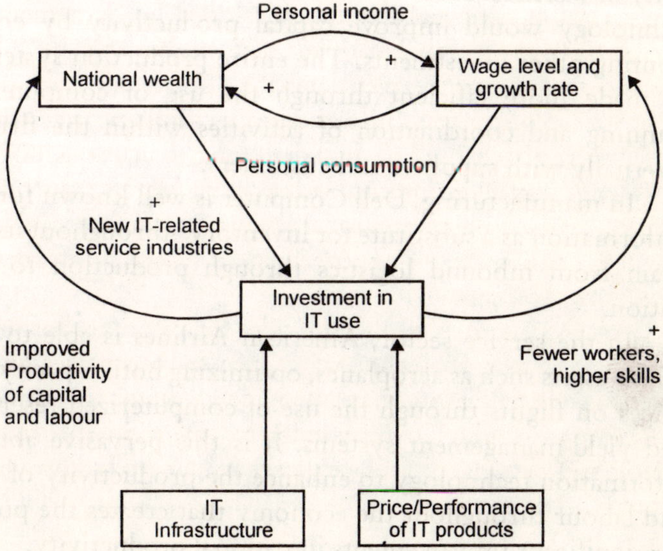

economic growth. Information technology use might also have a negative effect by leading to the elimination of jobs, but these losses should be compensated by new employment created by economic growth. Also, new jobs are created directly in the area of information technology use. These include user support, software programming, system integration and maintenance. Increased information technology use also creates new information-based business opportunities in the economy and in the information technology industry itself, especially in production close to use such as information services, thereby stimulating additional economic growth.

The key issue presented by the framework in Figure 1.1 is whether information technology investments result in improved national productivity, which is also the crux of the productivity paradox.

It is generally expected that information technology use will increase national productivity in two ways. First, information technology would improve labour productivity directly by substituting for capital or improving the productivity of workers. Second, it has been expected that information technology would improve capital productivity by complementing other investments. The entire production system can be made more efficient through the use of computers for planning and coordination of activities within the firm and externally with suppliers and customers.

In manufacturing, Dell Computer is well known for using "information as a substitute for inventory" throughout its value chain from inbound logistics through production to distribution.

In the service sector, American Airlines is able to better utilize assets such as aeroplanes, optimizing both capacity ticket prices on flights through the use of computerized reservation and yield-management systems. It is this pervasive ability of information technology to enhance the productivity of capital and labour throughout the economy that creates the potential for significant improvements in national productivity.

In short, economic factors and information technology investment are interrelated. On the one hand, the remarkable price/performance improvements in information technology over the last 20 years have stimulated companies and countries to invest more in information technology use with the expectation of improved productivity and economic growth. Information technology use can in turn enhance productivity and stimulate the growth of information technology-related industries, both of which will result in higher economic growth rates and better living standards.

Empirical Studies

The country level studies of the economic impacts of information technology have focused on the contribution of information technology towards GDP growth using time series economy-level data for a single country. A limitation of this approach is that capital and labour tend to move together with each other and with the scale of the economy, making it difficult to obtain reliable and statistically significant results with a single country. In order to minimize this problem and to draw meaningful conclusion about the impact of information technology investment at the country level, Matti Pohjola of UN University (2001) conducted an empirical study of multiple countries over time.

An important precursor to such cross-country analyses of information technology payoffs was an inter-country analysis using a growth theory approach conducted by DeLong and Summers (1991). The authors assessed the impacts of investments in machinery and equipment (M&E), and compared them to the impacts of investment in other types of capital.

They found that over the twenty-five year period 1960-85, each extra per cent of GDP invested in M&E was associated with an increase in GDP growth of one-third of a percentage point per year. This was much stronger than the relationship found with non-equipment capital, suggesting that M&E were more productive than other capital. That article provided a basis for differentiating returns on investment in different types of capital.

The first analysis of information technology investment across countries was conducted by Kraemer and Dedrick (1994), who used data from 1984 to 1990 for twelve Asia-Pacific countries that represented different levels of economic development. Information technology investment was defined as total spending for computer hardware, software and services within a country. The study found a significant relationship between growth and services within a country. The study found a significant relationship between growth rates in information technology investment and both productivity and economic growth at the national level. Owing to the limited data involved, it was not possible to employ more sophisticated models that would control for the impacts of other variables. The study did, however, identify several factors that were strongly correlated with levels of information technology investment, consistent with the model presented in Figure 1.1 These factors include wealth (GDP per capita), education levels, structure of the economy (share of employment in the services sector), and level of information technology infrastructure (telephone lines/100 people).

A recent and comprehensive inter-country study by Dewan and Kraemer (2000) uses production function analysis with data from thirty-six countries for the period 1985-93. The variables used in the analysis include: information technology capital (defined as computer hardware, data communication), and GDP per worker hour. Currency conversion are based on purchasing power parity, and capital (both information technology and non-information technology) is measured as stocks. Results are presented for the entire sample and for sub-samples of developed and developing countries, both cross-section and over time.

The analyses showed that the returns on information technology investment are positive and significant for developed countries, but not statistically significant for developing economies. The estimate of information technology output elasticity is 0.057 (positive and significant) for developed countries, but statistically indistinguishable from zero for developing countries.

These findings challenge the productivity paradox by showing that information technology makes a positive contribution to the economies of developed countries. A possible explanation for the substantial contributions in developed countries is that new information technology investments in developed countries can leverage off complementary investments in information technology infrastructure, human capital, and information-oriented business processes, as well as earlier information technology investments, to amplify the payoffs from information technology. It is likely that the impact of information technology must be attributable to the entire 'system' of complementary investments, as opposed to information technology alone. Accordingly, one explanation for the lack of significant returns on investments in lesser developed countries is the relative scarcity of information technology infrastructure and other enabling investments. It may also be simply that investment levels in information technology are too small to have a measurable impact on GDP.

New Empirical Research

Approach used by Kraemer and Dedrick (1994) can be deduced in two ways. First, the earlier empirical analysis of Asia-Pacific countries with a larger sample of countries over a longer time period. Second, a growth theory approach to the same sample.

The extended empirical analysis correlates growth rates in information technology investment with labour productivity growth for forty-three countries from 1985 to 1995. With this much larger sample, they are able to produce more robust findings than in the earlier study and also control for growth in non-information technology investment, as well as labour force growth and initial GDP per capita. Instead of simply measuring total information technology and non-information technology investment growth, however, they have chosen to use information technology and non-information technology investment per worker as the independent variables.

Conceptually, this makes sense because the dependent variable is growth in GDP per worker, and thus measuring the capital investment in the same terms. Initial GDP per capita is included in order to control for the possibility that poorer countries will inherently tend to have higher or lower growth rates. Labour force growth is included to control for the possible decline in productivity as new, inexperienced workers enter the labour force. The formula used by author is: Growth in GDP/worker = f (GDP/capita 1985, labour force growth 1985-95, growth in information technology investment per worker 1985-95, growth in non-information technology investment per worker 1985-95). The aggregate sample data are presented in Table 1.1.

Table 1.1

IT Investment and Labour Productive for 43 Countries from 1985 to 1995

Indicator (in millions)	*Mean*	*SD*	*Median*	*Min*	*Max*
GDP, 1995 in US$	522,106	1,243,636	155,371	12,366	6,952,020
Population, 1995	87	220	21	3	1,200
Labour force, 1995	43	118	9	1	709
IT investments, 1995 in US$	11,058	35,389	1,927	126	224,298
Per cent IT investment of total investment	7.5	4.6	5.6	1.6	19.4
Per cent IT investment of GDP, 1995	1.5	0.8	1.5	0.4	3.2
GDP growth, 1985-95 (CAGR)	3.0	3.0	2.5	-3.9	10.1
Labour force growth, 1985-95 (CAGR)	1.5	1.2	1.3	-0.5	5.2
IT investment growth, 1985-95 (CAGR)	17.3	5.8	16.0	8.0	33.1
Non-IT investment growth, 1985-95 (CGR)	8.2	7.3	9.0	-14.4	21.2
Productivity growth, 1985-95 (CAGR)	1.5	2.6	1.2	-3.9	8.3

Source: Adapted from Matti Pohjola edited book *IT: Productivity and Economic Growth*, Oxford 2001, New York, p. 264.

Growth in information technology investment per worker was calculated from data provided by International Data Corporation (IDC) on total information technology spending by country from 1985-95, divided by number of workers, from the International Labour Organization's Yearbook of Labour Statistics (1997).

Growth in non-information technology investment per worker was calculated by subtracting information technology spending from total gross fixed investment, from the World Bank's World Development Indicators (1997), divided by number of workers.

Results from the Cross-Country Analysis of Kraemer and Dedrick

- Based on information technology/worker, the relationship between information technology and productivity was positive and significant.
- Based on a growth theory analysis, there was not a significant relationship.
- Based on production function analysis, developed countries have shown a strong evidence of payoffs from information technology investment, while for developing countries there was no conclusive evidence.
- Returns to non-information technology investment were positive and significant regardless of the model applied.

The lack of impact of information technology investment in growth theory models was probably due to two factors. First, levels of information technology investment was small relative to non-information technology investment, as suggested by Sichel (1997). Only when information technology accounts for a larger share of total investment, we are likely to see statistically significant relationships. Growth theory approaches required longer time series than were available for their analysis (1985-95), in order to smooth out the effects of the business cycle. For example, DeLong and Summers (1991) use data from 1960-85 to show the impact of equipment investment.

It is unlikely that any particular empirical study will produce the incontrovertible proof of the payoffs from investments in information technology and silence all of the skeptics. Rather it is the cumulative evidence from a number of studies, using different methodologies and different data sets, that is building a stronger case for the value of information technology. Even the findings based on growth rates of information technology spending per worker, which includes data from forty-three countries over eleven years, is far more convincing than the circumstantial evidence upon which the productivity paradox was initially based.

Finally, and suggestive of what future analyses might hold, Dewan and Kraemer's most recent analysis holds, year-by-year regressions from 1985-93 which shows that the output elasticities of information technology are positive, and steady or increasing over time, whereas the elasticities of non-information technology capital are decreasing. Moreover, there is evidence that information technology investments have started to become productive for developing countries towards the end of the sample period. Thus, it appears that the important question for the future is not so much whether information technology investments pay off on average, but what factors determine the value of information technology at the national level, and what policies create the conditions under which the payoffs can be realized.

Payoffs from Information Technology Use

The evidence of empirical research shows that investments in information technology use are correlated with increased productivity and economic growth for countries, and that the relationship is clearest for developed countries. They have invested in information technology over a long period of time, have accumulated a substantial installed base, and have achieved positive and significant returns to information technology.

They also have made complementary investments in telecommunications and human resources which enable them to achieve these positive returns.

The logic of information technology returns for lesser developed countries is the same as for the developed countries. However, because these investments are small relative to total GDP, the information technology impacts is less obvious in some studies. The fact that a particular analysis does not find a significant contribution of information technology in developing countries does not mean that developing countries should shy away form information technology investments. On the contrary, it is possible that there is some threshold of information technology investment, or experience in use, that must be reached before these investments are measurable, or become as productive as non-information technology investments.

The logic of technology use suggests that even widespread diffusion of new technology in a country is not necessarily sufficient for the benefits to be achieved. The recipient country must have the right environmental conditions, such as basic infrastructure, business practices and government policy, which reinforce the technology's deployment. Historical studies of countries that have been particularly successful indicate that such policies include promotion of computer use, promotion of education generally and of computer professionals in particular, enactment of low taxes and tariffs on computer imports, and telecommunications liberalization to lower costs (Dedrick, Goodman and Kraemer, 1995; Dedrick, Kraemer and Choi, 1995; Kraemer et al, 1996).

The implication of these results is that developing countries can benefit by promoting information technology use and creating the environmental conditions needed to support effective use. This is an especially significant conclusion because many developing countries' policies now promote information technology production over use. However, the research on information technology use and related research on computer production (Dedrick and Kraemer, 1998) suggest that the economy-wide benefits from information technology use are likely to outweigh the benefits from production, which are limited to just one segment of the economy. The importance of information technology use is becoming amplified by the process of economic globalization, which puts a premium on information and communications systems as the means to achieve linkages to international markets and global production networks.

Globalization, Information Technology Use and Productivity

In order to benefit from globalization, and from foreign competition in the domestic market, developing countries need to establish competitive capabilities beyond cheap labour. These can take the form of educated workers, high quality infrastructure, local R&D capabilities, and strong entrepreneurial skills. Another competitive advantage is the ability to use information technology effectively. When markets are opened up, domestic companies face competition from MNCs who bring in the most advanced information systems. In order to compete, domestic firms can develop partnerships with those MNCs to gain access to the technology, as a number of Mexican and Brazilian banks and retailers have done in recent years. They can work with leading information services providers in order to develop their own systems, or in some cases they may decide to outsource their information systems altogether. Whatever strategy is used, staying competitive requires investments in information technology to develop world-class information systems.

In addition to staying competitive in the domestic market, companies that make these investments are also setting the stage for competing in international markets. The global production networks of many industries (for example, PCs, semiconductors, automobiles) are moving quickly to integrate the entire supply chain electronically. Electronic data interchange was a first step, but now MNCs are linking their design, procurement, manufacturing, logistics and marketing through Internet based technologies. Even low-technology industries such as textiles and footwear are following suit. Internet commerce will make it possible for even small companies in remote locations to market their products in these production networks and will need sophisticated information technology skills and good information infrastructures. Those that have made the investments and developed the capabilities will benefit from globalization, while others will be left out.

Production versus Use

Creating a local information technology industry, however, is not a simple matter, especially for newcomers to the industry. While a number of new countries entered the industry during the PC revolution of the 1980s other countries such as Brazil and Mexico had little success, and some earlier industry participants, including many European countries, were squeezed out. Even Japan and Korea have limited success in computers (as opposed to components) outside their own markets.

In anything, the opportunities for newcomers are more limited today. Industry segments such as microprocessors, operating systems and packaged business applications are virtually closed off because the standards are set by the leading players in information technology industry, mainly US companies such as Intel and Microsoft. Other segments of the hardware industry require large capital investments, economies of scale, and specialized skills that few countries can hope to achieve. Moreover, many of these opportunities have already been pre-empted by earlier entrants such as Singapore, Hong Kong, Korea, Taiwan, Ireland, and Israel. Only a newcomer with a large domestic market and proximity to an existing supplier base is likely to enter these industry segments. China is doing so by negotiating with multinationals for production and technology transfer in return for market access. It also happens to be located near the vast supply chain that spans East Asia. Some countries are offering expensive incentives to attract foreign investment in hardware production, but it is questionable whether they can catch up at this point. And even if they are successful in attracting foreign investment, the resulting industry is likely to have limited value added and few opportunities for local companies to participate.

Finally, production benefits only one industry sector – the information technology sector, while information technology use can benefit all industry sectors. So if local production is promoted at the expense of domestic users, for example through import barriers that raise process, the bargain is probably a bad one for the economy as a whole.

Given the choice between promoting production or users, it is better to argue for use, especially in countries that are not already part of the global production network of the computer industry: Fortunately, however, the choice does not have to be so stark in most cases. In fact, there is a policy option that simultaneously encourages information technology use while also creating opportunities to develop a local industry – that is, production close to use.

Production Close to Use

Most national policies to promote computer production have focused on hardware, which is the most tangible segment of the industry. However, the fastest growing segments of the computer industry for over a decade have been software and services (Table 1.2).

Table 1.2

Growth Rates of Different Segments of IT Industry, 1985-1995

Industry Segment	*CAGR (%)*
Hardware	11.0
Software	15.9
Services	20.9

Source: Report on the Computer Industry, McKinsey & Co., 1996.

The software and services industries offer some specific advantages over hardware production. First, while some parts of the software industry are dominated by multinationals, there are still many opportunities to develop niche products without competing directly with Microsoft, Oracle, SAP and other large companies. These can be products developed for local markets that meet the needs of local language, culture and business environments. The services business offers even more compelling opportunities, as services usually must be provided locally for users and providers, and can benefit both users as well as providers, helping countries realize the payoffs from information technology use.

Figure 1.2 shows how information services such as systems integration, outsourcing and network services can serve as a link between production and use. These linkages can help local users apply the technology more effectively, and can create business and employment opportunities for local people in developing countries. These businesses are specially appropriate for developing countries because there are lower entry

Figure 1.2

Information Services as Link Between Production and Use

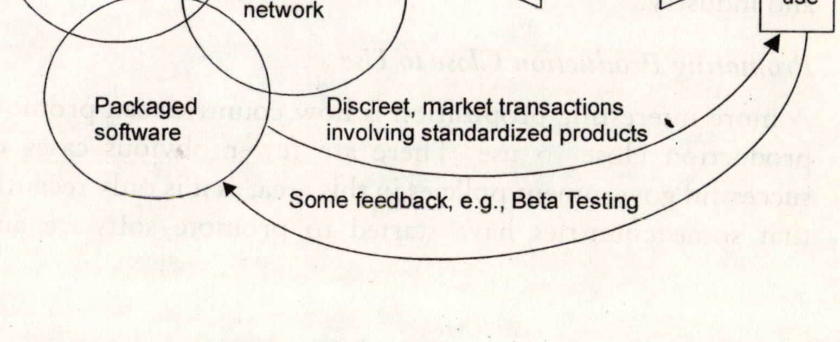

costs, so local companies can start small and grow at a pace that is supportable by their own finances and capabilities.

All of this does not mean that developing countries cannot participate in the hardware industry. In fact, as PC companies move towards build-to-order production, there are new opportunities for countries that have, or are close to, large markets. Those countries then may be able to attract suppliers to support PC production and create a competitive industry cluster for information technology production. But even those countries should not be so focused on hardware that they ignore the great potential of software and services. Countries just trying to enter the industry with limited resources to invest, should look carefully at whether efforts to promote hardware production would have the same payoffs as promotion of information technology use and production close to use.

Development Strategies

Effective national strategies to realize the benefits of information technology, need to cover three areas: promoting use, promoting production, and developing national capabilities. These policies are much more effective when they are closely coordinated and receive support from the highest levels of government, as is the case in Singapore and Taiwan. They will also be more effective when developed in close consultation with the private sector, including both local and multinational firms, and with domestic and foreign experts from academics and industry.

Promoting Production Close to Use

A more interesting proposition is how countries can promote production close to use. There are fewer obvious cases of successful government policies in this area, as it is only recently that some countries have started to promote software and services production. Also, most previous academic research on the computer industry has emphasized computer hardware or electronics more broadly. Only a few studies, such as Schware (1992) and Carmel (1995), have focused on the software industry. Perhaps the most valuable contribution to this area is Schware's notion of 'walking on two legs' which argues that countries should target production and use in tandem, focusing on the interaction between production and use in the software and services industries.

Schware's argument, which is expanded upon in Dedrick and Kraemer (1998) is that the interaction between producers and users is critical to the development of certain types of software and information services. The question is what types of policies can facilitate this interaction and provide resources needed by local companies to participate in these markets. Some recommendations suggested by authors are:

Promote Small Business Information Technology Use

A growing, sophisticated user base is the best resource for software and services companies. In particular, smaller vendors benefit from use by small business, who traditionally turn to those vendors to set up and maintain systems and networks, design web pages, provide Internet services, and design custom software to solve specific problems. An example of a policy to promote small business use and help local developers can be seen in Taiwan, where the government is helping software to solve specific problems. An example of a policy to promote small business use and help local developers can be seen in Taiwan, where the government is helping software companies develop applications for small business such as restaurants and bicycle shops, which often have multiple outlets. It is hoped that these applications can be eventually sold around the country and to Chinese language markets around the world.

Provide Financial Support

Software and services companies often fail to survive even when they have good people and technology, simply because they are starved for capital. Very few countries have well-developed venture capital markets or over-the-counter stock exchanges, and developing countries do not have many wealthy 'angels' who are familiar with the industry and willing to fund start-ups. Governments can provide or guarantee low-interest loans in relatively small amounts that are appropriate for small companies. They can also provide direct grants to promising companies. In both cases, the key is, having the capability to make sound judgments about the companies, business plans, management skills, and market prospects.

Encourage Partnerships Between Local Firms and Multinationals

One of the best ways for local firms to get established is to operate as subcontractors for multinational corporations. Local firms are often used for software localization and maintenance, product support, marketing, and other services. Working with world class companies helps develop the skills and knowledge needed to grow and compete, and also can provide a reliable revenue base to support that growth. Governments can offer incentives to multinationals to participate in partnership programmes, and also provide resources directly.

Developing Capabilities

In order to support both information technology use and production, countries need to develop capabilities in the form of human resources, information infrastructure, R&D, and business skills. At one level, there is a need to develop a broad base of basic capabilities, such as raising the level of education for the population as a whole, and putting in transportation and telecommunications infrastructure throughout the country. In the long run, information technology will benefit developing countries to the extent that they can achieve the widest possible diffusion of the technology, and create the broadest base of capabilities to support information technology use and production close to use. India has created a high-speed network in the Bangalore area, complete with satellite uplinks, to support the fast-growing software industry in the region.

Conclusion

As countries look at how they can realize the potential benefits of information technology, they need to weigh the value of promoting information technology production and use. While there are good opportunities to be found as a producer in such a fast growing industry, many segments of the industry are dominated by powerful incumbents and present very high entry barriers to newcomers. Attempting to enter such segments through protectionist policies is unlikely to succeed, and will exact a high cost to users by raising prices for information technology. Other policies, such as providing financial incentives to producers, might be more successful, but in many cases developing financial incentives to producers, get only little more than low value assembly operations in return for costly incentives. A few new countries might break into high volume hardware production, but most simply do not have the resources.

Fortunately, there is a segment of the industry that presents good opportunities for developing countries, while also helping to support better use of information technology. This segment, which consists of services and specialized software, is actually the fastest growing part of the industry, and offers many openings for small niche players.

Some of these niches might eventually grow into large markets, and those small players can develop globally competitive products and services. Such production close to use is a good fit for many developing countries, offering business opportunities for local firms and jobs for skilled information technology professionals who might otherwise have to go abroad to use their skills. The most effective policies for developing countries are those that promote use and production close to use, and those that build national capabilities (Kraemer and Dedrick, 2001). If these policies are developed in close consultation with the private sector and academic institutions, and if the efforts of related government agencies can be coordinated so that they complement, rather than compete with each other, the result can be a rapid diffusion of the technology, with broad benefits for the country.

2

Information Technology Scenario in India: Past, Present and Future

Information technology essentially refers to the digital processing, storage and communication of information of all kinds. The information technology can potentially be used in every sector of the economy. The true impact of information technology on growth and productivity continues to be a matter of debate, even in the United States which has been the leader and largest adopter of information technology. However, there is no doubt that the information technology sector has been a dynamic one in many developed countries, and India has stood out as a developing country despite the country's relatively low level of income and development.

In this chapter, the information technology scenario in India has been discussed under several sub-headings as below:

- Share of information technology output to gross domestic product (GDP).
- Share of hardware in information technology output from domestic segment.
- Share of software in information technology output from export segment.
- Share of information technology enabled service in export segment (NASSCOM as a guiding force of the Indian information technology sector is discussed).
- Gross revenue from information technology sector.

- Employment generation in information technology sector.
- Constraints/barriers to balanced growth of information technology.
- Policy initiative of government and its implications.
- Outlook for future.

Share of Information Technology Output to Gross Domestic Product (GDP)

India's experience with growth of the information and communication technology (ICT) sectors, especially the information technology component, has attracted attention for a number of reasons. To start with, the pace of growth has been rapid, albeit from a low base, tallying with the dynamism seen as typical of the industry and captured by the oft-quoted Moore's Law.[1] Thus, according to data provided by Dataquest, over the 12 years period 1990-91 to 2001-02, the annual compound rate of growth of output was 37.4 per cent.[2] That is, output was doubling every 2.2 years. The net result has been that the ratio of gross information technology sector output to GDP rose from 0.38 per cent in 1991-92 to 1.88 per cent in 1999-00 and to 3 per cent in 2001-02. It is evident from Table 2.1 and Chart 2.1:

Table 2.1

Indian IT Output to GDP Ratio

Year	*Output Growth (%)*
1991-1992	0.38
1995-1996	1.08
1999-2000	1.80
2000-2001	2.08
2001-2002	3.00

Source: Dataquest, http://www.gartner.com

The industry is gaining significance in the Indian economy with sustainable growth rates, increased contribution to FDI,

Chart 2.1

Ratio of IT Sector Output to GDP

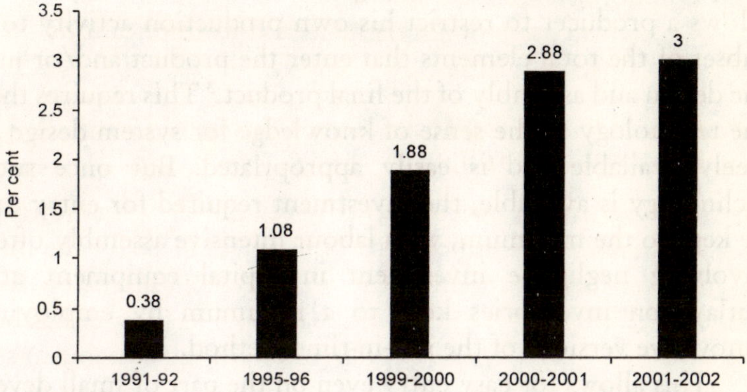

Source: Dataquest for IT Industry Output. GDP figures from Economic Survey.

employment and exports. This industry has led to wealth creation of Rs 90,000 crore in the last six years and is expected to attract cumulative FDI worth $ 1.2 billion by 2006 (NASSCOM).

Share of Hardware in Information Technology Output from Domestic Segment

In the hardware segment, the production of a range of products varying from components like printed circuit boards to peripherals like modems, on the one hand, and the assembly of personal computers, on the other, do not require large investments for entry. Many of these are heterogeneous products that can be put together on the basis of a combination of internally produced and externally sourced intermediates and components. There are no doubt some components entering into ICT hardware, such as the microprocessor, the production of which is capital intensive in nature, and dominated by a few global players like Intel, Motorola and AMD. But this does not preclude the presence of smaller players in important 'downstream'. The real 'technology' in these downstream areas is a system architecture that maximizes the benefit derived from an appropriate combination of subsystems, components and peripherals. That is, the heterogeneous nature of the product allows a producer to restrict his own production activity to a subset of the total elements that enter the product and/or just the design and assembly of the final product.[3] This requires that the technology in the sense of knowledge for system design is freely available and is easily appropriated. But once such technology is available, the investment required for entry can be kept to the minimum, with labour intensive assembly often involving negligible investment in capital equipment and outlays on inventories kept to a minimum by employing innovative versions of the just-in-time method.

This allows for easy entry even on the part of small developing-country producers and partly allows for the emergence of international brands from the developing world, as is true of Acer from Taiwan. What is crucial here is access to outsourced components ensured, *inter alia*, by a liberal import regime. This, the rapid growth of the PC hardware segment is seen as facilitated by the removal of quantitative restrictions and the reduction of tariffs imposed on imported components, even while restricting and keeping expensive end-product imports. As the domestic markets for PCs expands, domestic production of components becomes viable, resulting in the emergence of an information technology production 'complex', and a reduction in import intensity. However, while convincing as an idea, this process can be subverted by developments in the software sector, as happened in India.

When the domestic market for PCs and peripherals is relatively protected and component imports are highly taxed, the few large players coexist with the large number of smaller suppliers. It should be obvious that all segments of the domestic industry benefited substantially from the quantitative restrictions on PC imports, with premium producers garnering high margins and the lower-end assemblers surviving despite high costs and poor service support. Needless to say, the small assemblers with low margins were in no position to use the opportunity afforded by protection, to build capabilities of a kind that would allow them to compete with large international suppliers as and when protection was withdrawn. On the other hand, with the government not enforcing R&D based competitive production in the premium segment, and premium producers choosing to encash the large margins rather than plough them back into production, even they did not concentrate on developing indigenous sources of supply of components and accessories and on reducing costs and developing significant product innovation capabilities.

The effects of this history were seen when the government, eager to exploit India's capabilities as a software and information technology enabled outsourcer decided to ease access to and lower duties on information and communication technology products. The first casualty were some producers in the premium segment who when faced with the abolition of quantitative restrictions and the reduction of duties on a range of PC products, decided they could not face up to the competition. Some chose to become domestic sales agents for international brands. But almost all leading producers have substantially diversified out of PC production into software-generation.

As a result, in the wake of liberalization the industry has seen significant changes in structure. Liberalization has resulted in the gradual conversion of some premium producers into domestic sales agents for international firms. Wipro, for example, had virtually discontinued its own range of products and has become a supplier of Apple and Acer products. It has also resulted in the closure of at least some large volume retailers such as Sterling, though some other large producers like HCL have remained in the PC business. Finally, as the volumes sold by multinational brands increase and duties on imported components fall, there has been a growing threat of erosion of the market share of assemblers by these international suppliers.

Table 2.2

Major PC Vendors in the Domestic Market, 1999-01

Vendor	*Units 1999-00*	*Units 2000-01*
Compaq	79484 (2)	151568
HCL	1011500 (1)	149500
Hewlett-Packard	63000 (3)	91200
IBM	40534 (6)	67644
Wipro	49000 (5)	66699
Zenith	59685 (4)	60646
DELL	15500(12)	38000
PCS	17500(10)	36350
Vintron	20598 (8)	30575
Minicomp	27260 (7)	29271
Visualan	16570 (12)	23746
Acer	18000 (9)	22100
Apple	9000 (14)	12000
SNI	10000 (13)	10000
CMS	5000 (17)	8000
Computech	5893 (16)	8000
Accel	6480 (15)	7000
Others + assembled	580321	892736
Total	1125235	1705335

Source: Dataquest.

As Table 2.2 shows, in 1999-00, about a half of the top 15 PC brands in India were known international brands, there were only two major domestic players who were involved in retailing volumes larger than 50,000 PCs a year, and these producers were falling behind in the competition with transnational producers.

To quote Dataquest: "Gone are the days of PCL, DCM and ECI – the erstwhile heroes of the domestic information technology market have long vanished or have been relegated to history books. Today's domestic market is run by MNCs." Look around at any of the information technology segments in India and the frontrunners are likely to be MNCs. Think of servers and you think of Sun, IBM, Compaq and HP. About printers, you have to but think of HP, Epson and Samsung. On networking products, who can you think of but Cisco and 3Com? Sure, there are some lone Indian rangers, for instance HCL Infosystems in desktops and TVSE in impact printers, but even their numbers are fast dwindling. This is a domestic scene that is nearly monopolized by MNCs.[4]

The tendency for these transnational suppliers to source virtually knocked-down, resulting in a high and growing import intensity in the industry. This implies that the output and employment implications of the rapid growth of domestic hardware spending would be far less than suggested by the gross revenue figures. This reflects the unusual situation in the PC market in India, where despite a long record of PC production even by international standards, there are increasingly a few international brand names like IBM, Compaq, Dell and HP coming to dominate the market.

The core of the computing business is dominated by a capital-intensive and oligopolised product like the microprocessor, the market for which is dominated by a few producers like Intel, Motorola and AMD. And, the technologies driving a range of peripherals like printers and networking products, for example, are proprietary and are not replicated without a licence. This implies that hardware production in India amounts largely to assembly of components, much of which is imported. Indigenous content is restricted to certain of these components and indigenous technological input is confined to system architecture and design. As a result, value added domestically tends to be small.

Further, while capital investment requirements for production may be small, production for geographically and quantitatively large national and world markets require high sunk costs. This takes the form of initial expenditures on marketing, retailing and the creation of an after-sales service network. Deep pockets and/or access to large sums of capital are therefore a prerequisite for entry into this segment of the hardware sector.

This has implications for the linkage effects of the growth of the PC industry and for net foreign exchange earned by the information technology sector. Needless to say, with imported components accounting for a substantial share of the value of PCs assembled by both the international players and domestic assemblers, the domestic linkage effects of the growth of PC sales could only be limited. Much more employment is likely to be created by the growing demand for maintaining and servicing the installed PC base (estimated at 7.5 million). In the PC segment itself whatever value is added domestically would accrue in the hands of large international firms. Given the sourcing practices of these firms it is likely that the import intensity of PC production in India would remain high, resulting in the leakage of at least some of the revenues earned from exports of software and information technology enabled services.

These features of the PC market, which would be even truer of the peripherals market, indicate that, in the wake of liberalization, the emergence of a strong indigenous industry that engages world markets is not likely to be a substantial restructuring of the international industry in favour of developing countries such as India, at least so far as hardware production is concerned.

The domestic software industry clocked a revenue of Rs 11,500 crore in 2001-2002 as compared to Rs 9,890 crore in 2000-2001. The domestic industry growth rates declined in 2001-2002 to 16 per cent in 2000-2001. This is evident from Table 2.3 and Chart 2.2.

Table 2.3

Major Trends in Domestic Sectoral Spending from 1995-96 to 2001-02

(percentage)

Sectoral Spending	*95-96*	*96-97*	*97-98*	*98-99*	*99-00*	*00-01*	*01-02*
Private	53	51	76	66.2	69.3	66.0	73
Government	18	19	8	19.4	14.2	15.1	12
Public	29	30	16	14.4	16.5	13.9	15

Source: Dataquest.

Chart 2.2

Trend in Domestic Sectoral Spending

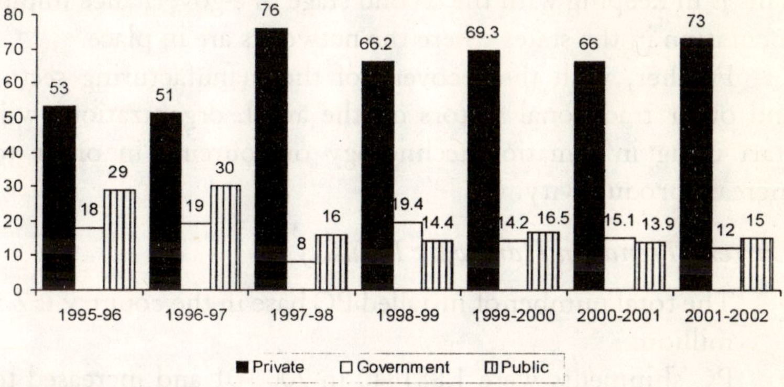

Source: Same as Chart 2.1.

Trends in domestic sector spending indicates that there is a consistent decline of government spending from 18 per cent in 1995-96 to 12 per cent in 2001-02. Whereas private sector spending increased from 53 per cent to 73 per cent during the same period. Thus, there is an urgent need to spend domestically more by the government.

However, there are a number of opportunities emerging in the domestic sector, which will help catalyze growth in the next 2-3 years. These include the energy sector, insurance, financial and banking services, e-governance and the manufacturing sector.

In the energy sector, deregulation will drive spending on Enterprise Resource Planning (ERP) and Supply Chain Management (SCM). Further, with the privatization of the power sector, spending on information technology to improve productivity will get an impetus. In the banking and financial service sector, the need for nation-wide connectivity and the imperative to improve customer access will provide opportunities for information technology. Also, the emergence of new insurance companies will lead to increased information technology spending.

For e-governance, the major thrust will have to be in the area of local language applications and application integration. This is in keeping with the second stage of e-governance implementation in the states where the networks are in place.

Further, with the recovery of the manufacturing sector and other traditional sectors on the anvil, organizations will start using information technology outsourcing in order to increase productivity.

Current Trends in Hardware Industry

- The total number of installed PC base in the country is 7.5 million.
- PC shipments were 1,881640 in 2000-01 and increased to 1,650,000 for 2002-03.
- The domestic information technology hardware market has grown 76 per cent over the last five years, from $1.7 billion in 97-98 to $ 3 billion in 01-02, but the segment has seen a gradual shift from indigenously sourced production in favour of imports.
- MNC brands maintained a robust performance – a market share of 36 per cent, up from 24 per cent in the first half of 2000-01, registering a growth of 44 per cent.
- Overall the PC purchases in the top four metros (Delhi, Mumbai, Kolkata and Chennai) accounted for 53 per cent of the total PCs purchased.

Share of Software in Information Technology Output from Export Segment

There has been a trend shift in the rate of expansion of information technology sector output, driven by exports. The trend rate of growth of output valued in dollars rose from 23.7 per cent to 29.8 per cent during 1991-1996 to 1996 to 2002, whereas the rate of growth of exports rose from 32.5 per cent to 46.6 per cent during the same period.

As a result, the share of exports in information technology industry output, touched a remarkable 61 per cent during 2001-02.[5] Thus, rapid growth of information technology sector has essentially been the result of a rapid expansion of exports. During the period 1990-91 to 2001-02, exports have grown at 54 per cent per annum or doubled every 18-24 months.

Segmentwise estimation of India's IT industry output reveals (Table 2.4) interesting results. In the beginning of 1990 it was the domestic segment which was contributing 80 per cent

Table 2.4

Segmentwise Estimates of India's IT Industry Output

(Rs. in crore)

Year	*Domestic segment*	*Per cent to total*	*Export segment*	*Per cent to total*	*Total*
1990-91	1762	80	452	20	2214
1991-92	2041	75	676	25	2717
1992-93	2524	73	931	27	3455
1993-94	3356	70	1405	30	4761
1994-95	4959	72	1882	28	6841
1995-96	7032	72	2681	28	9713
1996-97	8587	64	4847	36	13434
1997-98	10835	60	7180	40	18015
1998-99	13204	55	10752	45	23956
1999-00	17002	51	16050	49	33052
2000-01*	24670	45	29896	55	54566
2001-02*	24288	40	37846	60	62134

Source: Dataquest.

Note: * ITeS included in software exports.

Chart 2.3

Compound Annual Growth of Output by Segment 1990-91 to 2001-02

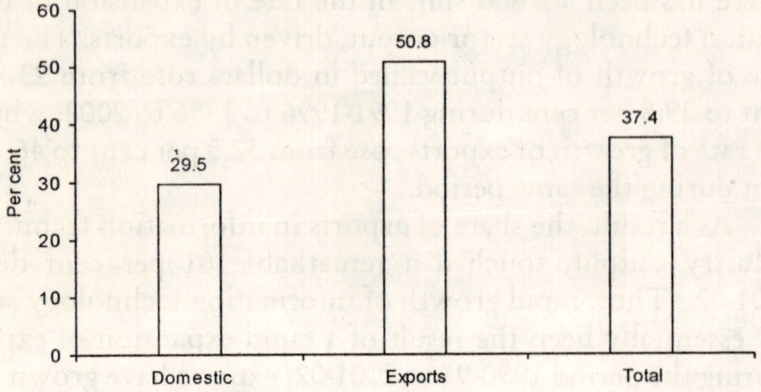

Source: Dataquest.

of total output while export segment was 20 per cent. On the other hand by 2000-01 contribution from domestic segment declined to 40 per cent while export segment increased to 60 per cent.

Table 2.5

India's Export Earnings in Billion Dollar (1991-2001)

Year	*Earnings*
1990-91	0.25
1991-92	0.28
1992-93	0.30
1993-94	0.45
1994-95	0.60
1995-96	0.80
1996-97	1.3
1997-98	1.93
1998-99	2.56
1999-00	3.70
2000-01*	6.54
2001-02*	8.04

Source: Same as Table 2.1.

Note: Rupee figures converted using average annual exchange rates reported by Economic Survey and RBI.

Chart 2.4

Compound Annual Trend Rates of Growth of Output in Dollars

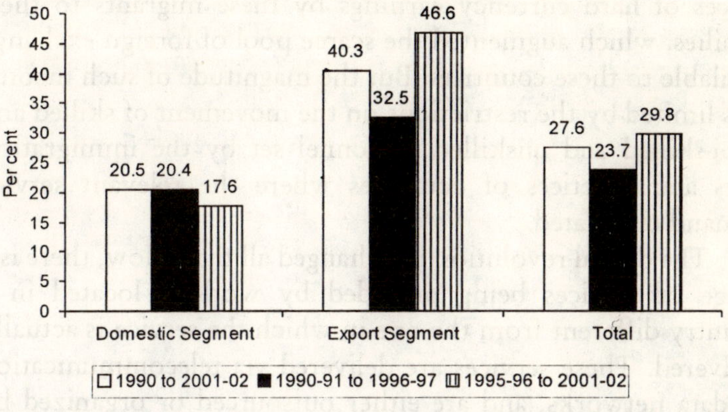

Source: Same as Chart 2.1, converted to dollars using exchange rates from various issues of Economic Survey.

In terms of export earnings in dollars, there is a tremendous accumulation of foreign exchange by export units. Table 2.5 and Chart 2.4 indicate that in the year 1990-91 hardly there was 0.25 billon dollar earnings. But by 2001-02 earning has reached 8 billion dollar. Thus, export segment has out smart the domestic segment in the Indian economy.

Share of Information Technology Enabled Services in Information Technology Export Segment

The third area where the information technology revolution has opened up whole new opportunities for India is in the information technology enabled services sector. Prior to the digital revolution's transformation of service activity, the provision of most services required the presence of a service provider at the point of delivery of the service. As a result, services export took the form of migration of personnel to the location where the service was provided, as epitomized by the migration of skilled technicians, doctors and nurses to the US and of semi-skilled and unskilled workers, including carpenters, masons, chauffeurs and housemaids to the Gulf countries from India. Benefits to the home country came in the form of remittances of hard currency earnings by these migrants to their families, which augmented the scarce pool of foreign exchange available to these countries. But the magnitude of such income was limited by the restrictions on the movement of skilled and semi-skilled and unskilled personnel set by the immigration laws and practices of countries where the relevant service demand originated.

The digital revolution has changed all that. Now, there is a range of services being provided by workers located in a country different from the one in which the service is actually delivered. These services are delivered via telecommunication or data networks, and are either outsourced or organized by agents in the country of origin of the service to whom the provision of these services are contracted out or out located by subsidiaries of corporations from the country of delivery of certain services. When categorized by origin and focus, it is possible to identify four types of information technology-enabled services (ITeS): in-house or captive centres, units that originally spin-offs, business process outsourcing (BPO) units and broad-based service provider, who offer consulting or information technology services in addition to BPO. Examples of services outsourced/out located include customer interaction services; the processing of credit card accounts, insurance claims and business payrolls; the creation and maintenance of information bases in the form of networked data centres and their use in the provision of information services such as help desks; and the generation of digitized records as in the case of medical transcription.[6] Other examples of out location include investment in design subsidiaries and back-office facilities.[7]

The possible range of information technology enabled services in an environment where the service sector's role is growing worldwide is immense. The reasons why such relocation occurs are obvious. It substantially reduces the cost at which such services are obtained or provided, and so long as an appropriate location in terms of the availability of manpower with the requisite skills (say, basic computer literacy) and the necessary characteristics (e.g., knowledge of English) is chosen, the quality and efficiency of the service is also ensured. The contribution of ITeS to total software exports indicates high performance.

Table 2.6

Contribution of ITeS to Total Exports from 1999-2002

(%)

Years	*IT-enabled Services*	*IT Services*
1999-2000	14.0	68.0
2000-2001	14.5	85.5
2001-2002	19.0	81.0

Source: www.nasscom.org

NASSCOM estimates suggest that revenues from information technology enabled services increased from Rs 2,400 crore in 1999-2000 to Rs 4,100 crore in 2000-01 and further Rs 7,100 crore in 2001-02. It has increased the share of information technology enabled services in the total revenues.[8] As a share of exports, NASSCOM estimates suggest that the contribution of ITeS rose from 14 per cent in 1999-2000 to 14.5 per cent in 2000-01 and 19 per cent in 2001-02 expectations are that ITeS would account of a much larger share in 2002-03 (Table 2.6). The IT-enabled services sector is highly diversified. It has shown tremendous growth during the last year and is turning out to be the second pillar of the Indian information technology export and employment.

NASSCOM as a Guiding Force

National Association of Software and Service Companies (NASSCOM) is an apex industry association in India. The member companies of NASSCOM are in the business of software development, software services, Internet, e-commerce and IT-enabled services. It was established in 1988 as a 'not-for-profit' organization with over 850 member companies. It represents 95 per cent of the total revenues of the information technology, software and services industry. It has played a vital role in catalyzing the growth of the information technology industry in India, whose revenues have increased multifold to US$ 15.8 billion in 2001-2002. It is credited with having positioned the Indian information technology industry in overseas markets as one that stands for an impeccable cost value proposition. It has actively networked with policy makers, industry players, technologists and academicians to propel the growth in the Indian information technology sector. It acts as a single reference point for overseas companies/ investors for setting up the operations/alliances in the ICT sector for investments.

The objectives of NASSCOM are:

- Maintaining close interaction with the government of India in formulating national information technology policies with specific focus on information technology software and services.
- Maintaining a state of the art information database of information technology software and services related activities for use of both the software developers as well as interested companies overseas.
- Encourage members to provide world class quality products, services and solutions in India and overseas and help build brand equity for the Indian information technology software and services industry.
- Taking effective steps to campaign against software piracy.
- Provide an ideal forum for overseas and domestic companies to explore the vast potential available for joint ventures, strategic alliances, marketing alliances, joint product development, etc., by organizing business meets with delegations of various countries.
- Work actively with overseas government embassies to make the visa and work permit rules more "India industry friendly".

- Disseminate various policies, market information and other relevant statistics by sending more than 200 circulars (annually) to all members.
- Involve membership participation in various forums of NASSCOM on subjects such as HRD, technology, exports, domestic market, e-governance, IT-enabled services, IPR, finance, government policies, quality, etc.

Gross Revenue from Information Technology Sector

Whether India is likely to emerge as an information technology powerhouse which invades developed country markets and challenges developed-country players is valid at all, it can only be true of the software segment. In information technology-related services it is the export market that provides the real opportunity. Table 2.7 and Chart 2.5 show revenues from services in the domestic market are currently close to a fifth of that from the export market, and the ratio of domestic revenues to export revenues fell from 42 per cent to 22 per cent between 1998-99 and 2001-02.

Table 2.7

Gross Revenue from Domestic as well as Export Earnings in Rupees from 1998-99 to 2001-2002

(Rs in crore)

Years	*Domestic*	*Export*
1998-99	4358	10306
1999-00	5690	15387
2000-01	7885	28730
2001-02	8065	36153

Source: Dataquest.

It is evident that gross revenue from domestic sector has doubled from Rs 4,358 crore in 1998-99 to Rs 8,065 crore during 2001-02, whereas gross revenue exports tripled from Rs 10,306 to Rs 36,153 crore in the same period.

Chart 2.5

Revenues from Services

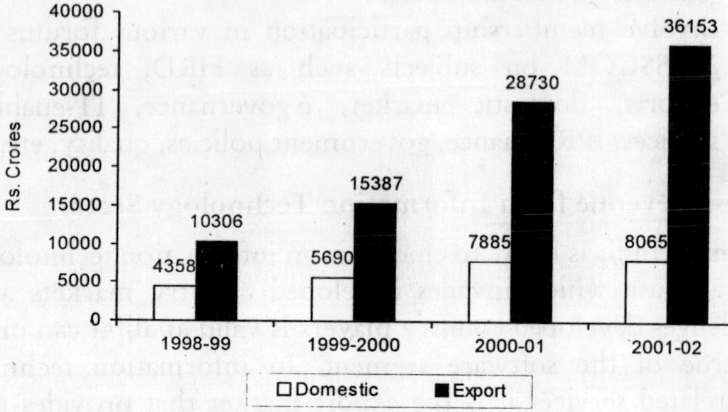

There are three broad categories into which such revenue services fall. 'Hardware services', including maintenance of the growing installed-base of computers; educational services, which generate the skilled and semi-skilled personnel needed to sustain information technology-sector growth; 'software services', including the production of software packages, generation of customized software; and the provision of a range of 'IT-enabled services'. In the domestic market, revenue from software services, at Rs 4,767 crore in 2001-02, was only about one-and-a-half times the combined revenue from hardware and educational services totaling Rs 2,743 as Table 2.8 and Chart 2.6 show.

Table 2.8

Structure of Revenue Earnings from Services: Domestic

Year	*Domestic Services*	*Export Services*	*Education Services*
1998-99	940	2224	194
1999-00	1182	2947	561
2000-01	1578	3978	2329
2001-02	1830	4767	1467

Source: Dataquest.

Chart 2.6

Structure of Revenue from Services: Domestic

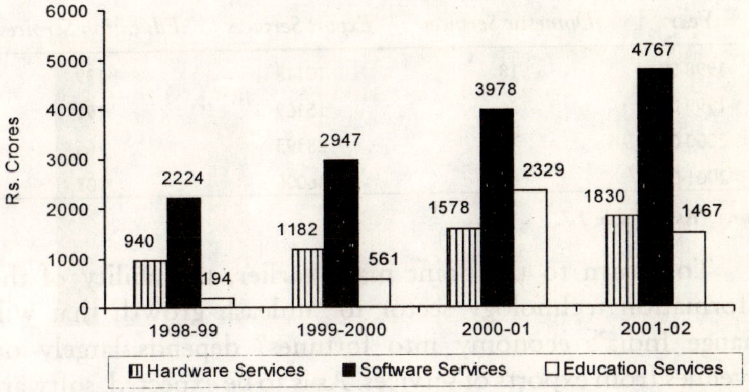

That is, not only were domestic service revenues small, but revenues from areas such as maintenance and the creation of basic information technology skills generated as much 70 per cent of the revenue garnered from the production of information technology enabled software.

This is of significance because a large domestic software services market provides the workplaces for training for software personnel and the base for generating the skills necessary to meet the higher demands of export market and to graduate to the higher end of the software value chain. That base is crucial since a substantial part of revenues from information technology-related educational services is known to accrue to teaching shops that do not develop adequate skills among its students. A growing disproportion between the market for domestic and export software services, therefore, constrains the ability of the system to generate the wherewithal in terms of the personnel needed to service the export market. This is the first factor to take account of when making judgements of India's potential in the export of software services.

Table 2.9

Structure of Revenue Earnings from Services: Export

Year	*Domestic Services*	*Export Services*	*Education Services*
1998-99	18	10148	139
1999-00	26	15169	191
2000-01	73	28393	265
2001-02	40	36006	107

Source: As in Table 2.7.

To return to the point made earlier, the ability of the information technology sector to "unleash growth that will change India's economy into fortunes" depends largely on revenues from exports of services. As is to be expected, software services and ITeS dominate the export of information technology services, accounting at Rs 36,006 crore, for more than 99 per cent of such exports (Chart 2.7). This is where the income and employment gains are going to be registered, as suggested by the fact that such exports grew by close to 50 per cent in 1999-00.

Chart 2.7

Structure of Revenue from Services: Export

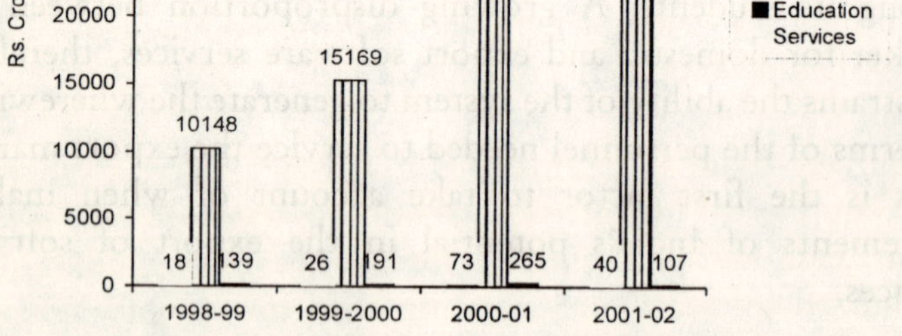

There are three prerequisites for the potential suggested by the above factors to realize itself. First, Indian software needs to diversify in term of sources and destinations. Of the 1,250 companies exporting software services in 1999-00, those exporting more than Rs 100 crore (about $22.5 million) stood at just 37. The top 25 exporters accounted for 61 per cent of exports revenues. And the US market dominated in terms of destination accounting for 62 per cent of exports as compared with Europe's 23.5 per cent.[9] Second, Indian software service providers should be able to sustain the quality of services offered by inducting appropriately qualified and skilled personnel to not merely write code but also design systems. Third, Indian firms should be able to migrate up the value chain, so as to ensure a growing share of the market as well as enter into segments that offer higher value per employee.

Table 2.10

Earnings from Different Types of Software Services

(Rs in crore)

Type	*1998-99*	*1999-2000*	*2000-01*	*2001-02*
Customized software	1924	825	1145	1603
Turnkey Projects	1815	944	1255	1650
Consulting/Others	979	456	547	725

Source: NASSCOM.

In all these areas the availability of personnel is bound to prove a constraint. The inadequacy of training services resulting from the proliferation of poorly-staffed, profit-hungry teaching shops, and the limited base for training and skilled-development in the domestic software services segment has already been noted. As a result even as an outsourcer, India still remains a lower-end software supplier and a supplier of information technology enabled services. As Chart 2.8 shows, unlike in the domestic market, generation of customized software or generating code for systems specified

Chart 2.8
Earning from Different Types of Software Services

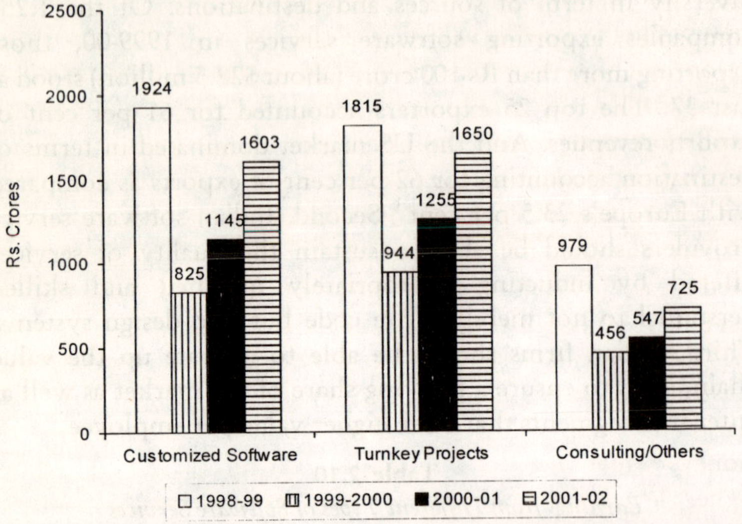

by clients dominates both the export software services market. As has been repeatedly emphasized, this often involves some body-shopping in the form of temporary export of software professionals to undertake specific jobs in large projects designed and executed in the West and enclave-type offshore supply.

Noteworthy is that even the big exporters obtained little by way of revenues from frontline software products or higher end consultancy and software generation services. To quote a senior executive from the Indian software sector: "India, somewhere down the line, has to make up its mind whether it would be a quality software developer or concentrate on quantity... if you look at the typical structure of the information technology services provided to any of the global companies – on the bottom layer is outsourcing, above it software development, on top of that is technology development and higher up is networking services and, finally, information technology consulting. As you move up, you get higher billing rates, higher revenues, higher gross margins and, thereby, high profitability because the complexity of the transaction is higher". Accordingly to industry insiders like Narayana Murthy of Infosys, this move up the value chain has hardly occurred and is not India's priority. In an interview, Murthy said Indian software expertise in customized services had a long way to go in quantity and quality before focusing entirely on other fields. "Yes, moving up the value chain is a good idea. We are at it ourselves – about Rs. 20 crore, which is just 8 per cent of our total business and not the main", he said[10].

He said India's share of the service industry – he calls it "customized software provision" – was only $2 billion. The market is a staggering $25 billion. India needs that kind of money, while there is no stopping it from reaching out to higher levels of technology. There are others, like Vinay Deshpande of NCore who feel that while software services should not be sneered at, the contract should be properly designed. "If the job is just another cover for body shopping, then there is little technology that accrues to the contractor."

Employment Generation in Information Technology Sector

Employment of software professionals in Indian information technology and ITeS segments has crossed 6.5 lakh by end of March 2003, reflecting a growth of 24.4 per cent over last year. The skills in demand are in the areas of software analysis, domain specialists, information security, integration specialists, database administration, communication, data warehousing and semi-conductor design.

Of the total, almost 2.05 lakh are working in information technology software export industry; 1.6 lakh are employed in ITeS segment, 25,000 in domestic software market and 2.6 lakh in user organizations. Hiring of new information technology professionals was highest in Southern states - Karnataka, Andhra Pradesh and Tamil Nadu at 44 per cent and lowest in eastern region at 6 per cent. As much as 79 per cent of software professionals were men. However, NASSCOM- 2002 study revealed that this ratio is likely to be 65:35 (male-female) by 2005.

In ITeS segment, about 65 per cent of total jobs were cornered by the women. The average age of professionals is 26.5 years. There was shift away from hiring fresher to professionals with more domain specific skill sets and business analysis with programming skills which reflects that Indian companies are tapping high value service lines. Multinational corporations and large Indian companies are major recruiters during 2003.

The advantage that India has in the information technology enabled services sector is obvious. But India's competitive advantages in the software export area are also many. To start with, outsourcing of information technology services is a dominant international business practice.

According to IDC, out of a global market of $220 billion for computer services in 1995, as much as $68 billion was outsourced. Outsourcing totalled $16 billion in the case of customized software development, $32 billion in systems integration, $11 billion in information technology consulting and $9 billion in business services. Compared with this, India's current (2001-02) exports of $8 billion of software services and information technology enabled services appears small. The opportunities are therefore substantial.

Second, till the recent slowdown in the information technology sector, the shortage of software professionals in the developed countries was expected to result in an increase in the share of computer services outsourced. Even though this would no longer be true, many argue that the need to cut costs during the downturn would accelerate outsourcing to countries like India.

Table 2.11

Employment Generation and Revenues from IT-Enabled Services

	1999-2000		2000-01		2001-02	
	Employed	*Revenue (Rs. crore)*	*Employed*	*Revenue (Rs. crore)*	*Employed*	*Revenue (Rs. crore)*
Customer Interaction Services including Call Centres	8,600 (19%)	400 (17%)	16,000 (23%)	850 (21%)	3,380 (32%)	1,790 (25%)
Back Office operations/ Revenue accounting/Data entry/ Finance and Accountancy	15,000 (33%)	950 (40%)	19,000 (27%)	1,350 (33%)	35,000 (33%)	2,850 (40%)
Transcription/Translation Services	5,000 (12%)	120 (5%)	6,000 (8%)	160 (4%)	6,200 (6%)	150 (2%)
Content Development/Animation/ Engineering and Design/GIS	15,000 (33%)	820 (34%)	27,000 (39%)	1,600 (39%)	30,000 (28%)	2,100 (30%)
Other services include Remote Education, Data Search Market Research, Network, Consultancy and Management	1,400 (3%)	110 (4%)	2,000 (3%)	140 (3%)	3,00 (1%)	210 (3%)
Total	45,000 (100)	2,400 (100)	70,000 (100)	4,100 (100)	1,07,200 (100)	7,100 (100)

Source: www.nasscom.org

Job-Switching in Indian Software (Labour Attrition)

A very high rate of manpower turnover is characteristic of the software industry in several locations in India. Job-switching across software firms ranged from 30-35 per cent (NASSCOM Report, 2003) in the early 1990s it was at least 25 per cent. The number of firms increased several fold, and several global corporations opened up their own units during this period in India. Manpower output with a software background also grew several fold. Inter-firm job-switching never came down during this entire decade, and a large number of personnel migrated to other global locations. All this indicates a market for software manpower, which had never existed before 1990, had come into existence in parallel with the emergence of the firms. This market, however, as we will soon observe, transacted mostly in experienced personnel.

Data on job switches were collated into a database created from the open advertisements that appeared during September 1998 to March 2000 in a popular Indian business magazine for the information industry. Data on a total of 1,615 advertisements for more than 10,000 jobs were covered. It should be noted that the total number of job switches is much higher than the advertisements indicate, since Indian firms induct a substantial fraction of their employees from the 'old-boys' network, and fresh employees are often recruited by large firms directly from the campus. Fresher without experience cannot provide the third type of information, although those who are recruited from the old-boys network and are from other firms do indeed provide information-in-expectation. Advertisements probe into the scope of coordination of expectations that the market can provide. These advertisements were in prose, and thus, the desired types of experience, qualifications or the advertised job positions had to be classified and clubbed together under several types. Only the years of experience required were given in exact numbers (Banerjee, 2002).

It was observed (ibid.) that skills requirements varied widely for the same type of job. Further, the nature of job-offers and the years of desired experience did not show any specific pattern (Banerjee, 2002). However, across almost all kinds of job-offers, persons with about up to eight years of experience appear to be in demand. Similarly, persons with up to eight years of experience in any specific areas are equally attractive in the job market. Contrary to popular belief, that in software experienced personnel tend to stick to the old firm, it shows that experience makes personnel even more attractive to the prospective employer.

It is not strange, therefore, that the high manpower turnover has not disturbed the growth in revenue, the market or in technology or innovative products. Instead, all the firms experienced growth in all these areas. The average sizes of all the firms also grew during this period. Manpower turnover, however, does affect firms in old types of industry which do not require coordination of their expectations on innovation. The knowledge management practices of such firms, as typical of a Japanese firm, emphasize tacit knowledge and knowledge located in job/tasks that is non-transferable (Nonaka and Takeuchi). A typical firm might then talk about lifetime employment and the firm's personnel practice would ensure restrictions on personnel mobility. Often such restrictions appear in the form of legally-binding clauses restricting floor-crossing through threats of penalty. Such penalties are imposed mostly on those employees who recruited as freshers and having spent substantial years with a particular job/task of a certain firm, acquire knowledge which has little market outside the firm, and conversely the firm, too, cannot replace that person with an experienced hand secured from the market.

Such a picture is missing in software; most software firms hire freshmen and put them through rigorous induction training followed by on-the-job training. A fairly large number of persons switch jobs immediately following such trainings, and this practice of job-switch is generally maintained by the person. Such trainings, however, are not given to new recruits with experience. Rarely would a firm apply strict legal rules in employment contracts, and there is no penalty ordinarily imposed on job-quitting. Software firms often retain a pool of extra manpower resembling the inventory of a manufacturing firm, and such a pool is either put on training in areas that the firm expects to develop, or is assigned to a development project/product. Upon thé sudden start-up of a new project, this pool is disbanded and works on the new projects. NASSCOM also conducted India's first ever city-wise survey on the ITeS sector covering 310 companies. The survey revealed that: the average number of employees in the ITeS sector is 190 but the range is huge and varies from as low as four people to as many as 16,000 people. The encouraging trend in this area is the presence of MNC captive units that account for 45 per cent of the industry and are a vital determinant of the long-term competitiveness of India in this sector.

Among the cities representing the ITeS sector, the National Capital Region (NCR) has emerged as the largest with 53 companies based in this region. Mumbai comes second with 45 companies and Bangalore and Chennai are at fourth place with 35 companies each. However, excepting for medical transcription, which records an abysmally low revenue per worker, there is not too much difference in the revenue per worker which averages Rs 6 lakh (or around $12,200) per year. This points to the fact that low wages do drive the industry. There are some unique issues facing the industry in terms of infrastructure, labour regulations, quality and manpower which need to be addressed to maintain the growth trajectory.

Constraints/Barriers to Balanced Growth of Information Technology

In understanding the constraints to the realization of balanced growth promise by advancing along the four routes to diffusion, there are four features of the structure of the information technology industry which are of relevance. These are:

- Private sector dominance in information technology investment and spending;
- Export dominance over information technology revenues;
- Software sector dominance over information technology revenues; and
- Export destination.

Private sector dominance in information technology investment and spending suggests that the nature of the capital stock and infrastructure generated and the pricing of most services that are offered would be largely governed by profit considerations. This would mean that infrastructure generation for provision of e-governance and information technology enabled social services delivery is not likely to result from the current dynamic of the information technology sector, but would need substantial state intervention. Evidence from other countries such as South Korea, which leads the world in terms of the spread of broadband connectivity, point in two directions: (i) the need for substantial state investment or state support for private initiative; and (ii) the existence of a 'killer application' (in this case gaming), if private initiative is likely to deliver such connectivity, even with state support. The level of per capita income and the experience with cable penetration suggests that such a killer application is unlikely to emerge in India in future.

The setback to domestic diffusion is all the greater because of the fact that India's information technology sector growth has been characterized by the dominance of export revenues over revenue growth. This does make the development of the sector take on an enclave-like character, with limited, even if not negligible, domestic linkage effects. It is not just that exports account for more than 60 per cent of information technology sector revenues today, but the fact that exports from software technology parks account for 80 per cent of software exports from the country. This would suggest that ICT expenditure would be concentrated in few locations, rendering the diffusion effects of ICT growth to be limited. In fact, an examination of the adoption of information technology by Indian industry based on ASI data indicates that only 35 per cent of factories covered in 1997-98 claim to use computers in offices, only 1.1 per cent have networked computer systems; just 3.7 per cent were connected to the Internet and a meagre 1.8 per cent used robotics or computerized processes in production.

Finally, diffusion is also limited by the fact that information technology sector growth in India is increasingly dominated by software revenues. It is not just that software revenues have tended to grow faster than hardware revenues, but the rapid growth of the software sector has generated a perverted form of the Dutch disease, adversely affecting hardware sector growth.

Initially the Indian hardware sector, which was more or less limited to domestic firms, consisted of three segments. Premium producers like Wipro, which controlled the market consisting of quality-conscious customer, who demanded a large and reliable after-sales services network and were willing to pay a higher price for these features. Large volume sales while limiting overhead costs and accepting lower per-initial margins. And a large number of assemblers with low overheads, a small employee-base and virtually no after-sales service, who catered to price-conscious customers willing to take quality risks. According to International Data Corporation (India), very small assemblers selling less than 200 units annually accounted for close to 5 per cent of the market for assembled PCs in 1998-99 (Table 2.12).

Table 2.12
Share of Market for Assemblers (Units Sold per year, 1998-99)

(in per cent)

Size	*Share of the market in unit terms*
A (more than 1000)	21.60
B (401-1000)	14.30
C (201-400)	15.60
D (up to 200)	48.50
Total	100.00

Source: IDC (India) website.

These small producers most often used inputs obtained from suppliers who had managed to evade customs duties. This reduced their costs substantially. Besides, these firms were satisfied with extremely low margins. As a result their prices were much lower than that of the large domestic suppliers. Not surprisingly, the market catered to by the assemblers as a group was by no means small. For example, during the first six months of 1998-99, PC assemblers accounted for a 53 per cent share of units sold in the Indian market and a 45 per cent of that market in terms of value.

The large premium producers defended their prices on the grounds of being technologically superior, of offering better quality and of providing far more reliable after-sales service facilities. In practice, having invested much in marketing to build their brand images, these large suppliers used the protection afforded by the government to garner large margins on their sales, but did little to build brand loyalty in the domestic and international market. Neither did the government intervene to ensure that the period of protection was used to build technological capability and viable sales volumes.

The third feature of the information technology sector's growth is that it has been driven largely by the private sector on both the supply and demand sides, though government support in terms of information technology infrastructure investments, duty free access to hardware for software exporters and zero taxation of export profits played a role. Almost all information technology firms producing for the domestic and international markets are private firms accounted for a dominant and rising share of domestic information technology spending since 1995-96 and contributed as much as 73 per cent of the total in 2001-02, as compared with 15 and 12 per cent by the government and public sectors respectively.

The fourth feature of the information technology sector growth is regarding the exports destination. Out of the total software exports of Rs 36,500 crore during 2001-02, almost 63 per cent was to the Americas (USA, Canada and Latin America); 26 per cent to Europe; 4 per cent to Japan; and 7 per cent to Rest of the World. USA continues to be India's largest export destination for more than a decade. Currently, more than 270 Indian companies have set up offices, subsidiaries and marketing alliances in USA.

An interesting trend in 2001-02 was the increase in software and service exports to USA, despite the slowdown in the US economy. Kiran Karnik said, "while the information technology services segment witnessed a slowdown in exports to USA, increase in ITeS exports to USA, resulted in an increased share of USA in India's software and services exports". The survey also saw Indian companies actively expanding into emerging markets such as Europe and Asia. Exports to Europe saw an increase of 2 per cent from 24 per cent in 2000-01 to 26 per cent in 2001-02.

Barriers to Entry in Software

What could be the source of barriers to entry in the software sector. Consider, for example, the packaged software segment, mass-producing branded products for large national and international markets. Knowledge products like software packages have the public good characteristic of non-rivalry in consumption, since making the product available to one user does not preclude its availability without much additional cost to another. This essentially implies that so long as the producer and seller of that knowledge can ensure excludability, or that sale of the product to one does not lead to the replication of that package for free use by another, there are substantial increasing returns in the software sector. Producing the first unit of a software product requires large investments in its generation, whereas producing an additional unit is almost costless. The larger the sales, therefore, the lower is average cost and the higher the return.

But that is not all. When large sales imply a large share of the market as well, scale becomes a means of ensuring consumer loyalty and strengthening oligopolistic positions. This is the result of 'network externalities' stemming from three sources. First, consumers get accustomed to the user interface of the product concerned and are loath to shift to an alternative product which involves some 'learning' before the features of the product can be exploited in full. Second, the larger the number of users of a particular product, the greater is the compatibility of each user's files with the software available to others, and greater the degree to which files can be shared. The importance of this in an increasingly networked environment is obvious. Finally, all successful products have a large number of third-party software generators developing supporting software tools or 'plug-ins', since the applications' program interface of the original software in question also becomes a kind of industry standard, increasing the versatility of the product in question without much additional cost to the supplier. These network externalities help suppliers of a successful software package to 'lock-in' consumers as well as third party developers and vendors, leading to substantial barriers to entry.

With the government failing to direct the sector in appropriate direction, the persistence of the current growth trends in the industry depends on India continuing to exploit the possibilities of arbitrage generated by differences in custom software and information technology enabled service costs between onsite sources and offshore centres. There is, however, some uncertainty as to whether India can do so. That possibility is threatened not merely by the emergence of alternative offshore centres in countries like the Phillippines and Israel, but also by a reduction in the onsite-offshore cost differential. First, is an inadequate pace of generation of additional and appropriately skilled software professional. Second, the 'suction-effect' exerted by software centres in the developed metropolitan countries. Learning from the success of Indian software engineers in Silicon Valley and elsewhere in the US, the United States government itself and governments in other developed countries like Germany, France and Japan are selectively relaxing their immigration laws and rules and quotas regarding the provision of work permits, to facilitate the flow of the best Indian software engineers to their countries. The attraction of the better salaries, lifestyles and work conditions in these environment ensures the rest. This has had some adverse consequences in India. To start with, it has raised the salaries paid out to top-end software professional close to international levels, reducing the cost advantage India had in this area. Second, it has created an acute shortage of highly-qualified, top-end experienced and skilled professionals in the Indian market for software engineers.

The prognosis with regard to India's migration to the higher-end of the software supply chain based on its knowledge-advantage is, therefore, not altogether positive. That movement is possibly as structurally constrained as the effort at increasing sophisticated manufactured exports from the developing to the developed world. It is for such reasons that optimistic projections of the kind emanating from the McKnsey/NASSCOM stable should be taken with more than a pinch of salt.

Policy Initiative of Government and Its Implications

The development of information technology is remarkable for two reasons: (i) they have occurred in a policy environment very different from those which characterized the import substitution years, and have therefore been taken as indicators of the positive effects that policies emphasizing private initiative and a minimalist state can have on growth; and (ii) since they are resulting in a noticeable increase in India's share of world software and information technology services production and export, they lend credence to the view that the information technology sector, besides being among the most dynamic areas in the global economy, is one where the new opportunities afforded are available to small and marginal firms.

The rapid growth of software services exports from India, as noted earlier, suggests that India has the managerial ability to exploit its competitive edge. The number of Fortune 500 companies that are outsourcing their software requirements to India has steadily grown to 185. The number of software exporting companies has also grown to 1,250.

Further, it is clear that a growing share of this export revenue is little more than the sale of cheap skilled and not-so-skilled information technology enabled labour services whose output is transmitted via modern communication technologies to sites where those services are required. The possibility of such service delivery has helped India circumvent the obstacle to service exports created by immigration laws in the developed countries. That is, a large part of software exports is not very different form the exports of nursing, carpentry, masonry and other such services, except for the fact that unlike those exports, the presence of the service provider the point of sale is not required in the case of information technology enabled services.

Thus, conceptually, India's software thrust of the last decade is not as spectacular as it appears. It is substantially export of lower-end software and information technology enabled services facilitated by the availability of cheap skilled labour. And it is in large part technology-aided extension of the earlier waves of migration by service-providers of different descriptions: doctors, nurses, and blue-collared workers of various kinds. An expansion of that kind cannot be self-sustaining. Even in quantitative terms the latter development is not spectacular. The 'net foreign exchange revenue' to the country from migration of the old kind, captured by the volume of remittance into India, is in the range of $10-12 billion. The gross foreign exchange revenue from software exports is, even after the boom, placed at $8 billion (Joseph, 2002).

The difficulty is that, the move up the value chain may not be a matter of pure choice, but structurally limited. While there have been instances of Indian companies delivering high-end products, like the banking and e-commerce software product, the industry generally accepts that much of the exports from India consists of low-end outsourcing and information technology enabled services. This limited success in terms of the composition of exports may be because there indeed are barriers to entry into higher-end software, resulting from the fact of increasing returns in the form of sharply reducing costs as volumes increase, helping create and strengthen oligopolistic positions.

Appropriating the Benefits of New Technology

Take the case of software products for mass use, for example, creating such a product starts with identifying a felt need (say, for a browser once the Internet was opened up to the less computer savvy or for a web-publishing programme once the Internet went commercial). The persons/firms identifying such a need must work out a strategy of generating the product, by hiring software engineers, at the lowest cost in the shortest possible time. Once out, the effort must be to make the product a revenue generating profit centre. The investment required is the sums involved in setting up the company, in investing in software generation during the gestation period, and in marketing the product once it is out so as to quickly win it a large share of the market. Needless to say, while entry by individuals or small players are not restricted by technology, they could be limited by the lack of seed capital. This is where the venture capitalists enter, betting sums on start-ups which if successful could give them revenues and capital gains that imply enormous returns.

There are however, three problems here. The first is one of maintaining a monopoly on the idea during the stage when the idea is being translated into a product. The second is that of ensuring that once the product is in the public domain competitors who can win a share of the market before the originator of the idea consolidates her position do not replicate it. It is here that a feature or 'entrepreneurial technologies' – the easy acquisition and widespread prevalence of the knowledge base needed to generate new products – considered and advantage for small new entrants actually proves a disadvantage. Thirdly, no software product is complete, but has to evolve continuously over time to offer more features, to exploit the benefits of increasing computing power and to keep pace with developments in operating systems and related products. Thus, large and financially strong competitors, even if they lag in terms of introducing a product 'replica', can in time lead in terms of product development, and erode the pioneer's competitive advantage.

There are two aspects of technology that are crucial in this regard. First, their source. Second, the appropriability of a technology. As mentioned earlier, in industries with routinized technologies, the source of technology was in significant part the activity of incumbent firms themselves. On the other hand, in the case of entrepreneurial technologies the sources were in the public domain. This was where the advantage lay for the small operator. But once a technology is generated based on some expenditure in the form of sunk costs, there must be some way in which the innovator can recoup these costs and earn a profit as incentive to undertake the innovation. In the Schumpeterian world this occurred because of the 'pioneer profits' that the innovator obtained. The lead-time required to replicate a technology itself provides the original innovator with a monopoly for a period of time that generates the surplus which warrants innovation.

Most often this alone is not enough to warrant innovation and in the software sector lead times can be extremely low, especially if the competitor invests huge sums in software generation, reducing the lead-time substantially. It is for this reason that researcher have defended and invoked the benefits of patents, copyright and barriers to entry in production, which allow innovators to stave off competition during the period when sunk costs are being recouped. Unfortunately, neither is the status of patents and copyrights in the software area clear (as illustrated by the failure of Apple to win proprietary rights over icons in user interfaces), nor are there barriers to entry into software production.

This has two implications. First, the importance of secrecy in the software business. The 'idea' behind the product must be kept secret right through the development stage, if not competitors can begin rival product developments even before the original product is in the market. A feeble attempt to institutionally guarantee such secrecy is the now infamous 'non-disclosure agreements' which prospective employees, financiers and suppliers are called upon to sign by the innovator who is forced to partially or fully reveal his idea. Second, even after the product is out, since the threat of replication remains, it is necessary to strive to sustain the monopoly that being a pioneer generates. This is where the possibility of locking in user with the help of an appropriate user interface which they become accustomed to and are reticent to migrate away from, and locking in producers of supportive software with an appropriate 'applications programming interface' becomes relevant.

It should be obvious that sustaining monopoly to recoup sunk costs can indeed be difficult.

Such strategies did help the early start-ups, resulting in the jeans-to-riches stories (Microsoft, Netscape, etc.) with which Silicon Valley abounds. But more recently it has become clear that start-ups undertake innovative activities only to create winning products that the big fish acquire. This is because of the possibility of easy replication and development of an original product, which can be done by dominant firms with deep pocket that allow them to stay in place and spend massively to win dominant market shares. In the event, the likelihood that a small start-up would be able to recoup sunk costs, clear debts and make a reasonable profit is indeed low. Selling out ensures that such sums can indeed be garnered. And selling out is often a better option than investing further sums in developing the product now faced with a competitive threat, in keeping with industry and market needs.

Given this feature of the software products market, it is not surprising that small players (such as Netscape with its Navigator and Vermeer Technologies that delivered Front page) are mere transient presences in key areas even in the developed countries. To expect developing country producers to fare better is to expect far too much. The latter can merely be software suppliers or outsourcers for the dominant players. This implies that, given the current trends in the industry, even on the software front the promise of ICT contributing to a redressal of even national let alone international, inequalities in technology and income is unlikely to be realized. The digital world seems to adding to and even worsening the existing divide.

Further, the promised expansion in exports as a result of the restructuring of commodity production by liberalization has not been realized despite ten years of reform in India. In the circumstances, the fact that the new sectors offer a combination of employment opportunities and export revenues from hardware, software and information technology enabled services, renders them the leaders in the effort to make globalization the appropriate means to enhance growth in output and employment as well as to reduce balance of payments vulnerability.

As mentioned earlier, in the past, the special characteristics of the information technology sector, which substantially reduce technological and financial barriers to entry by small players, were seen as underlying the success of small Silicon Valley start-ups. Those start-ups not only challenged traditional giants like IBM, but also have since grown to become major players in their own right and have changed the structure of the industry. The growth of the information technology industry in India and elsewhere in the developing world and India's success as a software exporter, seem to suggest that these characteristics hold for firms in developing countries as well. Not surprisingly, it is now being argued that what was true for the Silicon Valley start-ups in terms of their ability to break through barriers to entry should be true for the developing countries. It is this perception that underlies the optimism that information technology heralds a new era of reduced international inequality.

However, it is suggested that the rapid rates of growth of turnover in the industry should be treated with caution. Gross revenues are obviously misleading in the domestic industry segment characterized by substantial dependence on imported capital goods, components and software, especially in the hardware and packaged software sectors. With hardware and packaged software accounting for a significant share of domestic information technology, their high import intensity would substantially reduce the domestic multiplier effects of such spending.

There are a number of reasons to expect import intensity to be high. The domestic industry does not generate much packaged software, so that a substantial part of spending on this account would amount to leakage from the domestic economy. According to Dataquest, Indian companies launched 92 software products and updates in the domestic market in 2000-2001. However, MNCs launched 152, and dominated the market in most segments.

Microsoft's Office Suite, for example, occupied over 80 per cent of the market. Even in the case of hardware, import intensity tends to be high, especially in the servers, workstations, networking hardware and peripherals. In the case of single-user system two developments are likely to have increased import intensity over time. First, liberalization of component imports and reductions in import tariffs would have encouraged all producers to increase the share of components outsourced from abroad. Second, import liberalization and the relaxation of regulations on foreign firms, has increased the share of major international players in the domestic PC market.

However, it is not only in the domestic segment that there is a case for caution, if not skepticism, when assessing the larger international and national consequences of information technology growth. The discussion of the dominant export segment also suggests that there are not only difficulties in ensuring the appropriate 'diffusion' through growth of this kind, but also that the sustainability of such growth is not altogether certain.

Information Technology Growth and Need for Further Role of State

These features of information technology growth not only suggest that the high expectations from the information technology sector were in part misplaced, but that private responses to market incentives do not ensure the requisite changes in terms of technological development and brand-banding the hardware sector, the spread and appropriate diversification of software export activity, the adequate generation of software skills and the much-needed migration up the software export value chain. This points to the need for some intervention by the state not merely to facilitate such changes but enforce compliance along these lines on the part of the private sector. Unfortunately, the prevailing perception is that ICT-based industries are best left to private initiative and private responses to market signal. Any attempt at regulation has been interpreted as an effort to throttle the dynamism of private sector led growth. Accepting that perspective, the Indian government has increasingly withdrawn from regulation of this sector and has even offered substantial fiscal incentives and tax concessions, especially to the exporters of software and information technology enabled services. Besides implementing and proposing to implement a zero duty regime on a range of information technology products, the government has exempted profits from software service and information technology enabled service exports from payment of income tax.

On the other hand, in its role as facilitator, the government has taken on a range of responsibilities including that of ensuring the expansion of educational services so as increase the supply of information technology professionals and investing in and creating conditions for the rapid expansion of the information technology infrastructure, especially the availability of high speed links and international gateways with sufficient bandwidth.

This policy slant has had three consequences. First, it has meant that the government has not been able to ensure adequate technology absorption and development in the hardware sector. Second, the government has not been able to intervene to ensure the moving up the value chain of India's software industry. And, finally, the government has not been able to mobilize adequate revenues from what is a rapidly growing sector, even though it is required to undertake expenditures and investment to facilitate the growth of the sector, especially its export segment, as well as to seek to widen access to information technology. This is crucial given the fact that information technology is not all benign. As one analyst puts it "there is a clear risk that without policy intervention, ICT will intensify social divisions rather than close the same. The unregulated market is likely to develop information technology to address the needs of the better educated, wealthier, and more technology literate individuals, communities and countries, since these are the people who want and will be prepared to pay for the development of new and more sophisticated products and services".[11]

Outlook for Future

The Indian software services industry will witness an increase in addressable market in terms of new geographies, new service lines as well as higher penetration in new geographies that will provide growth opportunities for India to include Germany, France and Italy in Europe; Singapore, Korea and Malaysia in South-East Asia; and Chile, Mexico, Uruguay and Brazil in Latin America. On the service-lines front, Internet Subscribers outsourcing, application outsourcing and systems integration will be the growth areas. Among them healthcare, retail, government, utilities and telecom service providers are likely to increase their share in the total exports.

In future, Indian information technology software and service companies will have to work towards beefing up their capabilities. In the area of marketing, Indian companies will have to look towards building expertise through Leadership, gaining better customer access and key account management.

Indian companies will have to examine the possibility of building 'global delivery models' to overcome geo-political risks. Further, the industry will see a strengthening of domain expertise due to lateral recruitment.

Companies will try to contain costs by recruiting in line with utilization rates, hiking the proportion of variable pay, and better management of fixed price contracts.

International Data Corporation (IDC) View on Indian Information Technology Future

The information technology training market has been growing on double digits. The market witnessed a spurt in active players in the boom period and then quite a few of them opting to exit, hence the top players consolidating at the cost of the smaller players. The market will undergo interesting trends once the economy rebounds. The bulletin information technology Training market in India will understand these trends along with market size and future forecasts, players segmentation and other relevant details of the market. Internet subscribers will grow at 27 per cent between 2001 and 2006. The ISP sector is expected to witness a healthy growth in the coming years. The total number of subscribers is expected to grow at a CAGR of 27 per cent. It is expected to reach 8.2 million by 2006 while the revenue is expected to reach 35.5 billion by 2006, growing at a CAGR of 25 per cent.

According to V. Shekhar Avasthy, Assistant Manager, Internet, Communications and Convergence Research, IDC India: "The growth in the market can be contributed to falling PC prices, which eventually leads to higher PC penetration, which leads to higher Internet penetration, coupled with a drop in the access rates. Bandwidth usage in India will increase as prices come down." To substantiate this point, he cites the example of Videsh Sanchar Nigam Limited (VSNL), which has recently announced a 35-40 per cent cut in the rates of international bandwidth.

One of the most important happenings is the partial privatization of VSNL and the emergence of Bharat Sanchar Nigam Limited (BSNL) as a corporate entity. This enhances the competitiveness of the government owned agency and ushers a new era of competition in the Indian ISP market. MTNLs CLI based Internet access had a massive adverse effect on all ISPs and this is likely to change the business models altogether. While category 'A' ISPs have 90 per cent of the total subscribers, category 'B' and 'C' lag far behind pointing to the fact that shakeout in this has already happened (SatishYadav). Increased competition in the basic access market is driving the ISPs to look at alternate revenue models. Consequently, the ISP market in India is undergoing a transformation from high volume, low value to low volume high value services. These models are primarily driven by revenues from managed network services, e-commerce, security and content applications. The latest phenomenon in the Internet access market is VoIP, with some players launching new services for VoIP and rest studying the viability of these services. The value-added services that have picked up are the VPN and web hosting services. Most of the ISPs have different services offerings and the pricing is based on the number man-days required, number of location of access and web space used.

There is no standard definition of 'broadband' in the industry and IDC defines any connectivity of over 128 kbps as broadband connectivity. In case of broadband connectivity, while the market is still dominated by xDSL, cable-modem connectivity has not picked up as expected. However, the fact that even in case of business establishments that have the broadband connectivity, the actual output available to an individual user is too less, perhaps in proximity of 1 kbps per user. Thus in Indian context, the basic definition of broadband should be changed, for in the current scenario, the end user still faces paucity of bandwidth despite being on a broadband connection! The lack of applications that necessitate faster connectivity and cost sensitivity of Indian users keep the home users away from broadband connectivity.

The IP telephony has generated a lot of interest due to the Internet telephony being legalized in the country. The first to enter the Internet telephony market are the ISPs, which have introduced pre-paid calling cards both for corporate, as well as residential segments. The impact of the Internet telephony being legalized would be more in the ISD market than in the STD market. In India, only the PC to PC calls are allowed whereas the PC to PC and the PC to phone calls are only allowed for calling outside India. IDC expects the revenues of Rs 1802.5 million in the year 2002 to grow at a CAGR of 140 per cent to reach Rs 59.4 billion in the year 2006. The traffic is estimated to grow from 334 million MOU at a CAGR of 133 per cent to 9,838 million MOU in the year 2006. Value added services like Internet Data Centres, IP telephony are expected to become key revenue generators for ISPs and amongst various modes of Internet access, broadband will experience the fastest growth in the years to come.

Conclusion

In brief, the fallout of the above analysis to the realization of the potential of ICT is the following:

Despite its rapid growth the information technology sector in India is small and marginal and the fallout of its growth on the rest of the economy is limited. There are signs that barriers to entry outside the realm of production in both the hardware and software segments are substantial. This has adverse implications for sustaining the growth of both output and employment in this sector, unless the disproportionality in growth between the domestic and export segments is addressed and firms strive to strengthen domestic hardware production and move up the value chain in software. This requires the state to play a more proactive role in influencing the pattern of growth of this sector, rather than leave matters to the market which drives firms in the direction of the lower-end of the value chain, where entry is easier and profits quick to come by.

Despite the rapid growth and high profitability of leading firms in the software and information technology enabled services sector, the notion is that this is a sector whose growth is best left to the revenues garnered by the states. This substantially erodes the ability of the state to sustain even its role as facilitator (which involves large investments in the communications infrastructure), let alone providing funds to expand its role in the area. The industry must contribute out of its large profits, a part of the revenues to meet the much needed expenditures by the states in this area.

The state's role is the more crucial when we examine the prospect of sharply widening digital divide within the economy. Even beginning to provide access to the new technology to the overwhelming majority, who cannot access it for technological reasons would impose a large financial burden. But the more difficult task is to prepare the disconnected to develop the competence to participate, however marginally, in the emerging digital economy. This alters priorities completely. With literacy and schooling achievements still at indefensibly low levels, the first task of the government would be to rapidly advance the pathetic reach of literacy and school education in the country. In terms of priority this should be placed above the target of providing a minimum degree of access to ICT to those who are completely disconnected. However, the nature of the challenge of overcoming backwardness is such that a degree of syncopation is inevitable, necessitating large resources which in part must come from the surpluses being garnered by the rapidly growing and highly profitable information technology services sector. Thus, the growing dilution of the state's role in the growth in the information technology sector could aggravate the tendency to widen the 'digital divide' between India and the developed industrial countries, especially the US, and within India itself to persist and even widen. This strengthens the argument that the buoyant and the highly profitable private sector has to be treated on par with the 'brick-and-mortar' economy and taxed to generate the resources for such expenditures.

This need to push for greater expenditure by the state, is in the interests of the industry as well, for two reasons. To start with, a widening digital divide can only widen social divisions and tensions. Easy access to ICT enables people to become richer and therefore more able to afford still newer technology; it is moreover the already educated who disproportionately take up lifelong learning activities and who, in general, get better services. In short, the educated information rich become richer and less educated information poor become poorer.[12] No democratic society can tolerate growing divisions of this kind, making effective state intervention an effective policy option for the industry as well. Second, as the infrastructure and the capacity to participate in the transformation being wrought by ICT expansion – it not only expands the market for the domestic industry but also allows it to use the large domestic market as the base to generate the skills and develop the capability to move up the value chain in both hardware and software production.

State as facilitator will not do justice to all. There is urgent need of partnership between state and private. The public-private partnership (PPP), alone can meet the challenge that the information technology revolution sets for India.

Notes

1. This refers to the observation made by Gordon Moore as early as 1965 that newer chips that entered commercial production every 18-24 months incorporated twice the number of transistors as their predecessor.
2. In this paper three different sources of information are used: *Dataquest*, NASSCOM and IDC.
3. In India, for example, the Centre for Development of Telecommunications (C-DOT) designed, developed and patented a switching system more suited to environments characterized by low telephone densities and low call densities than is the case with switching systems imported from abroad. Much of the hardware needed for these rural automatic exchanges was sourced from other domestic producers or imported from abroad.
4. "Multinationals in India: Domestic Champions", *Dataquest*, July 31, 2001, p. 194.
5. This includes exports of IT-enabled services (ITeS) in the values for 2000-01 and 2001-02.
6. Medical transcription meets at low cost the need set by the medicare system in the US for detailed patient treatment records. Doctors

dictate the relevant entries and the spoken word is digitized and transmitted to locations in India where they are immediately transcribed into word processed files that, given the time difference between two countries, is available to the doctor concerned the very next morning for correction and finalization.

7. The McKinsey-NASSCOM report lists ten processes as attractive opportunities-telesales/telemarketing, Web sales and marketing, database marketing/customer analysis, benefits administration, payroll services, engineering and design, inbound call centre, claims processing, billing services, and credit/debit card services.
8. According to *Dataquest*. At present, the ITeS market in India is restricted to call centres. Even if some activity has taken place in other areas such as medical transcription, engineering and design or other Web services, this is seen as being too little to make a significant impact on the overall market or growth. "IT-Enabled Services: India IT's lone crusader", *Dataquest*, July 2002.
9. "Software Sales on Hard Drive", *The Economic Times*, July 4, 2000.
10. R. Mohan, "Products vs Services: The Argument Continues", *Business Line*, December 17, 1998, p. 7.
11. Stephen McNair, "The Emerging Policy Agenda" in Organization for Economic Cooperation and Development, Schooling for Tomorrow: Learning to Bridge the Digital Divide, Paris: OECD, 2000, p. 10-13, Stephen McNair, op. cit., p. 10.
12. Stephen McNair, op. cit., p. 12.

3

Software Technology Parks in India and Their Role in Software Exports

On the lines of special economic zones and 100 per cent export-oriented units, the software technology parks have been established by the Ministry of Communication and Information Technology, Government of India in 1991, with the objective of encouraging, promoting and boosting the software exports from India. Software technology parks aim to keep India the most preferred nation for software exports, with a twin endeavour of keeping cost of operations low and in the view of developing multiple centres for software exports. Many cities and towns have been identified as 'software hamlets'.

The software technology parks scheme is for the development and export of software, using data communication links or by physical media or by onsite consultancy. Software technology parks act as the front-end on behalf of the Government of India to take care of all the statutory needs, like project approval, import approval, bonding, software export certification, etc. The following are the benefits expected to be availed by the software exporters in India:

- Approval under single window clearance mechanism
- Duty-free imports of hardware and software

- Corporate income tax exemption up to 90 per cent
- 100 per cent foreign equity participation
- Exemption of excise duty for domestic purchase of capital goods
- Reimbursement of central sales tax
- Domestic tariff area (DTA) shall be permissible up to 50 per cent of export value terms
- Capital goods eligible for depreciation subject to a maximum of 90 per cent
- Issue of green card
- Second hand capital goods may also be imported
- Certification of software export made through data communication

In order to avail software technology park scheme's benefits, the minimum export obligation of the firm is US$ 0.25 million or three times of CIF value of imported capital goods, whichever is higher, and Net Foreign Exchange Earning (NFEE) of 10 per cent. This condition has became a little hurdle for small units in remote software technology parks. As a result number of units registered are less (for example, in Manipal software technology park there are only four units registered to avail the benefits). However, software technology parks supports new companies by providing incubation infrastructure with all facilities, viz., Internet, telephone, fax, photocopies, power back-up, etc.

Cyber Park: Technology Incubation Centre

The incubator concept has emerged world wide as an essential component of the infrastructure required for the growth of high technology businesses including information technology and software development. These incubators provide the necessary help to nurture technology ideas into commercial successes. These incubators, which traditionally acted as institutes for the creation of cutting-edge technology through technology transfers from universities, have become the centres of attention once again, this time in the developing countries.

It is also necessary to differentiate between the traditional information technology (and/or science) parks and the incubator facilities. The major differentiating factor is the availability of intellectual and financial support through a select consortium, which provides strategic advice regarding all business related issues. In the Silicon Valley most of the technology intensive companies are the start-ups by the young professionals who are supported by the angles at the initial stage, incubators from the infrastructure point of view and venture capital fund at the later stage. It is noticed now a similar effect has started in Bangalore and the 'cyber park' would greatly help in the bringing the Silicon Valley start-up environment to India.

It would also encourage the Indians and start ups to own the intellectual property (IP) within India. Till now most of the intellectual property that was developed in India has been owned by the US companies. The Cyber Park Technology Centre would provide the right environment for the start-up companies, so that they will encourage to own the IP and create India centric companies. All the infrastructural and communication will be hassle free to the entrepreneurs so that we can focus on the core knowledge development. This incubation centre would also have the relationship with the technology incubation centres that are functional in Ireland, Israel, US and Japan and would have a strategic relation with the angle funds and venture capital funds. As and when each industry grows beyond a stage, it will have some commercial space available in the same park so as to expand the operations. The Cyber Park incubation Centre is now managed by group of professionals supported by STPI, government and industry veterans in Karnataka.

Cyber park will have an integrated infrastructure of size 3,00,000 sq ft, in the land available with STPI while 75, 000 to 100, 000 would be required as incubation, to other block users available for entrepreneurs' growth as commercial base. The greatest advantage for this kind, of central facility is the co-located 'international gateway' facilities which otherwise could involve many other agencies to extend such communication services to the industry that are going to be located in the premises. This cyber park provides the following facilities:

Modular built-up area for ready to use by the software entrepreneurs, back-up power supply, telephones and fax facility, air condition, common canteen facility, business centre, banking services, hardware support and services, courier services, clubhouse and recreation Inc, travel-house conference rooms and training facilities, high speed communication links, Internet and video conferencing facilities.

Table 3.1

Statewise General Profile of the Software Technology Parks in India as on March 2003

States/UTs	*Centre (main)*	*Year of establishment*	*Sub Centres in each state*	*Number of units regd.*	*Software exports in crore*	*Percentage to the total %*
Andhra Pradesh	Hyderabad	1991	5	820	3638	10
Chandigarh	Mohali	1998	–	100	–	–
Delhi	Delhi	–	–	885	2065	6
Haryana	Gurgaon	–	–	161	2734	7
Karnataka	Bangalore	1990	4	1154	12350	33
Kerala	Thiruvananthapurum	1991	–	188	165	0.4
Maharashtra	Navi Mumbai	1998	4	757	5508	15
Orissa	Bhuvaneshwar	1990	–	152	260	0.6
Tamil Nadu	Chennai	1995	5	865	6305	17
Uttar Pradesh	Noida	1991	5	1103	2541	7
West Bengal	Kolkata	1995	–	131	1200	3
Other States			12	–	410	1
Total			35	6316	37176	

Source: 1. www.indiastat.com, 2. www.nasscom.org, 3. www.soft.net

Catalyst Role of Software Technology Parks

Today, in India, there are more than 7,400 software exporting companies operating under the umbrella of STPI. The share of the software exports by software technology park units is more than 80 per cent of the total software exports from the country. The statutory services are supported on robust intranet platforms to ensure instantaneous response to customer requirements. The service delivery is bound with definitive timeliness and toned with understanding of the best practices in the industry. As on 31st March 2003, STPI had set up 35 software technology park centres in the last twelve years.

Regarding the history of STPI, the first software technology park was established in Bangalore in 1990 with few software units that were already existing. Similarly, software technology park in Bhuvaneshwar was also established in 1990 in Orissa. Due to lack of infrastructure, availability of human resource (information technology skilled personnel) and lack of government full support, the software technology park, Bhuvaneshwar could not succeed in increasing its share in the total software of the country. As on 2003, it had exported only Rs 260 crore worth of software as against Rs 12,350 crore by Bangalore software technology park, which accounts for 33 per cent of share in the total software technology parks exports in 2003. Similarly, the export of software from Orissa software technology park is only 0.6 per cent. It indicates that performance of software technology parks depends on several factors:

(a) Supply of information technology skilled (English-speaking) workers which the Karnataka is able to supply due to existence of large number of information technology related colleges, established even before software technology park came into existence;
(b) Government's conducive policy due to information technology savvy Chief Minister; and
(c) Infrastructure availability like bandwidth, roads, water supply, etc.

On the other hand, Chennai software technology park was established in 1995. Its progress is tremendous in terms of number of units as well as amount of software exports within a span of eight years. As on 2003, it has exported Rs 6,305 crore worth of software, sharing 17 per cent of total exports next only to Bangalore. This progress is again attributable to the existence of a large pool of information technology skilled workers, infrastructure and conducive policy of the government in the state. Next highest share is from software technology park, Navi Mumbai with 15 per cent of total exports and Andhra Pradesh with 10 per cent of share in the national exports.

Though software technology park in Kolkata was established in 1995 along with Navi Mumbai, its share is only 3 per cent (though recently it has picked up). Being a Metro city, its share could have been more, but due to lack of conducive state policy in the early 1990s and insufficient information technology skilled (English speaking) workers it had to drag its feet. Now, the government of West Bengal has realized the necessity of English-speaking information technology skilled workers and thrust has been given recently in its policy.

As far as North India is concerned in terms of number of units registered under Noida software technology park (which also established in 1991), it is second highest but its share of exports is only 7 per cent, much below the share of software technology park, Bangalore and Chennai. This leads us to conclude that there are inherent comparative advantages in south than in north. Among the several advantages it is the supply of information technology skilled (English-speaking) labour that is needed and still generating lot of heat in certain states. Since 1980s, in the states of Karnataka and Tamil Nadu, there was a craze for establishing engineering colleges which made them to be the leaders in information technology exports, followed by Andhra Pradesh and Maharashtra.

Table 3.2

Statewise Software Exports through STPI Registered Units during 1998-99 to 2002-2003

(Rs in crore)

States	*1998-99*	*1999-00*	*2000-01*	*2001-02*	*2002-03*	*Average for five years total*	*Average five years growth rate (%)*
Andhra Pradesh	574	1059	2017	2805	3638	2019	20
Delhi	475	795	1100	1750	2065	1237	20
Haryana	180	405	1450	2140	2734	1382	22
Karnataka	2888	4321	7475	9904	12350	7388	119
Kerala	44	67	141	159	165	115	2
Maharashtra	529	1534	2570	4603	5508	2949	48
Orissa	53	89	200	213	260	163	3
Tamil Nadu	748	1874	2956	5014	6305	3379	55
Uttar Pradesh	674	1220	1660	2000	2514	1614	26
West Bengal	96	150	250	604	1200	460	7
Others	39	93	232	331	410	221	4
India	6,300	11,607	20051	29,523	37176	20931	338

Source: 1. www.indiastat.com, 2. www.nasscom.org, 3. www.soft.net.

Thus, role of software technology park varied from state to state depending on the support and cooperation of the state governments and the information technology savvy Chief Ministers. The software exports by software technology park units has risen by 700 times from Rs 17 crore in 1991-92 to Rs 11,607 crore in 1999-00. The cumulative annual growth rate (CAGR) of software exports under software technology park scheme over these years has been about 125 per cent. In terms of analysis across the states, it is again Karnataka which is leading followed by Tamil Nadu, Maharashtra and Andhra Pradesh. The average growth rate of software exports over five years period for Karnataka is 119 per cent, followed by Tamil

Nadu with 55 per cent, Maharashtra 48 per cent and Uttar Pradesh 26 per cent, and Andhra Pradesh 20 per cent of the total exports of software in each state during 1998-99 to 2002-03.

National Software Exports and Software Technology Park Units' Export Performance

As far as export performance of software technology park units when compared to national total software exports is concerned, there is tremendous progress made by software technology park units in the country. Their success can be gauged with the following figures. During 1992-93, all software technology park units put together have exported only Rs 52 crore worth of software accounted merely 8 per cent of national software exports. But, by 2002-03, within ten years they have exported Rs 37,176 crore and its share has jumped from 8 per cent to 81 per cent in the national software exports. This indicates that such a phenomenal progress was mostly due to special status of software technology parks enjoying benefits of 100 per cent EOU and also due to removal of restrictions of numerous regulations which the old economy industries do still suffer from.

Thus, software technology parks in India have played the role not only as a catalyst but also as a propagator of information technology culture in the cities of Indian economy. Thus, we can conclude that "had there been no software technology parks, Indian total software exports of Rs 46,100 crore (3% of GDP) could not have been made possible by 2003".

From the Table 3.3, it is evident that software technology parks have a lion's share in the total software exports of India during the last several years. It is due to the infrastructure facilities at the software technology parks as well as a close contact with all government departments that enabled the software technology parks to contribute to the national exports. Small and medium enterprises (SMEs) constitute nearly 61 per cent of the software industry. The contribution of these SMEs to the overall exports is mere 14 per cent. However, during

Table 3.3
Statewise Growth of Exports from STPI Units and Share in the National Total Software Exports

(Rs in crore)

Year	*Exports from STPs*	*Percentage to the total*	*National total software exports*	*Percentage share*
1992-93	52	0.0	675	8
1993-94	117	0.1	1,020	12
1994-95	246	0.2	1,535	16
1995-96	727	0.7	2,520	29
1996-97	1,780	1.6	3,900	46
1997-98	3,424	3.1	6,400	54
1998-99	6,300	5.7	10,940	58
1999-00	11,607	10.5	17,150	68
2000-01	20,051	18.1	28,350	71
2001-02	29,523	26.6	36,500	81
2002-03	37,176	33.5	46,100	81

Source: Same as in earlier tables.

2003, their presence was felt and their contribution has improved. The encouraging trend is that SMEs below Rs 50 crore have also witnessed 19 per cent growth which is above the industry average of 17 per cent in information technology services, products and technical services segment. Tier 1, third party companies and MNC back-ends in this segment have also grown at 26 per cent and 31 per cent respectively, which is above the industry average (Karnik, 2003).

SMEs sector is very important to focus on the technology performance. In India, SMEs sector is a major player and one of the reasons for its success is reasonable equity benefits in terms of distribution income. A strong SMEs sector is critical in terms of the services that it can provide to the larger enterprises and to the medium enterprises. In the developed countries, the SMEs have been performing well and the similar pattern is observed in advanced developing countries. It is also a known fact that in the developed countries, the large-scale enterprises are increasingly down sizing and depending on the network of SMEs. Hence, the technology strong SMEs system in developing countries will be essential to develop, attract and work with larger enterprises.

Software companies feel that software technology parks efficiently acts as a nodal agency for most of their financial, legal and regulatory approvals, besides offering office space, connectivity and advisory services during the initial stages. The feeling is that software technology park can effectively lobby with the state and the central government for crucial issues faced by the industry. Dependency of large software players on STPI is restricted to Customs and some legal clearances as they are able to meet their infrastructure needs on their own. Smaller players continue to depend on STPI for their infrastructure needs. N. Natraj, director at Aztec Software points out, "STPI is one of our prime vendors, it has provided us with our Internet link, besides setting up our disaster recovery site." Staying up-to-date with developments in technology, especially with respect to streamlining connectivity, is an important aspect that software technology parks needs to improve upon. Manoj Bawa, finance controller at Talisma says, "software technology parks can streamline its connectivity as its uptime is not so good, which has made us look for alternatives in the form of private service providers who give us guaranteed uptime. If uptime is not good and efficient, it can affect the business of a company". A few players found a tie-up with private players as an answer to software technology park's connectivity problem.

Measures Planned by STPI

Setting up New Software Technology Parks

So far, the larger cities have the benefit of better infrastructure and have a major role in software exports from the country. Of late, a large number of units in the information technology enabled services sector have been set up in India. Smaller cities, who have the advantage of lower costs can play a major role in this sector. Most ISPs are not setting up communication infrastructure at secondary location because of commercial considerations. STPI may set up additional software technology park centres with centre/state government support at secondary locations, which will contribute to the export of information technology services.

Fibre-Landing Station by STPI

The availability of bandwidth through satellite is not very high. DoT has recently announced the landing policy of submarine cable. It is felt that few submarine fibre cables are likely to land in Chennai, Mumbai, Cochin and Vizag. STPI is already providing the data communication through its satellite earth stations. Due to the growth of information technology software export segment, the software companies also need bandwidth through fibre. Some of the companies, that are doing mission critical applications like call centre operation, security services, etc., require fibre to avoid transition delay inherent in satellite link.

Export Promotion

At present, the major share of software export market is in Europe and US. The smaller companies are unable to garner market share due to lack of market knowledge and ability to leverage their abilities in spite of inherent skills in product development and management. Such a situation, if continued, could confine them to very low growth rates for future. Accordingly, STPI has to plan to increase its focus as business promotion through increased participation in exhibitions, trade fairs and delegations, etc., for the SMEs sector.

STPI, Bangalore, is the first and largest contributor to India's software exports and scores over other STPI units in terms of the expertise and the services it provides. The credit for making Bangalore the information technology hub of the country goes to STPI in a large measure as it has taken a number of initiatives to boost information technology growth in the city. Over the years, STPI has become more prominent. The days when Bangalore had only a handful of software companies are long gone. There is still scope for further improvement in its functioning, especially when it comes to playing the role of a one-stop shop and in its ties with other government departments.

Software industry in Bangalore has been growing at the rate of around 60 per cent every year. Presently, there are more than 750 companies registered under STPI scheme in Bangalore. Apart from this there are another 30 per cent of the companies which are not registered under STPI scheme, but still engaged in the software export activities. These exports are also doubling every year. Besides this, the STPI has to play an important role in providing VSAT connectivity to the Government of Karnataka's e-governance projects. The Government of Karnataka is also using STPI's VSAT for its disaster recovery services, particularly in the treasury project.

There is no doubt that government bodies like STPI are inextricably linked to the growth of the software industry in India. STPI's praiseworthy help to the Karnataka government in assisting the state implement its information technology initiatives reveals the capability of STPI.

STPI is also in the process of building a strategic tie-up with one of the International Long Distance Operators (ILDO), which will help in providing services to call centres. STPI, Bangalore project itself, as a complete service-oriented organization, helping the information technology industry to effectively address communication management, information technology management, disaster recovery and business continuity issues. Thus, the role of software technology parks in Indian information technology sector is commendable. It has put its impression by a indelible ink in the map of information technology development of the country.

4

Tax Exemptions, Concessions and Relaxations for Information Technology Sector

The Government of India has announced information technology sector as a thrust area. Accordingly, it is providing for more liberal policy framework for the sector. Major laws and regulations that affect the information technology industry are discussed in this chapter.

One of the major factors of excellent and consistent growth of Indian software industry can be attributed to continuous liberalization of policies of both the Centre and state governments. NASSCOM and the government have worked together in close cooperation over a long time for forming and implementing these policies. During 1991, NASSCOM lobbied with the government and for the first time, secured income tax exemption from profits of software exports. Later, the government systematically and gradually reduced import duty on computer software from a high of 114 per cent to nil. Copyright laws were also amended. Some of the fiscal and non-fiscal incentives provided by the Government of India to information technology software and services industries are given in succeeding paragraphs.

Customs Related Issues (Exemption from Customs Duty)

The Department of Revenue, Ministry of Finance, Government of India has exempted the following goods from customs duty:

- information technology software;
- document of title conveying the right to use information technology software; and
- CD-ROMs containing books of educational nature, journals, periodicals or newspapers.

For this purpose, information technology software has been defined as under: "information technology software means any representation of instructions, data, sound or image, including source code and object code, recorded in a machine readable form and capable of being manipulated or providing interactivity to a user by means of an automatic data processing machine." Further, the above mentioned goods are also exempt from special additional duty.

Units in EOU/EPZ/STP/EHTP can donate (at zero import duty) computers and peripherals after two years of import and use to recognized non-commercial educational institutions, registered charitable hospitals, public libraries, public funded research and development establishments, organizations of Government of India or government of state or union territory. Duty is also exempted on import of second-hand computers/computer peripherals received by schools as donation from a donor outside India.

Income Tax Exemptions

As per the provisions of section 80HHE of the Income Tax Act, 1961, deduction in respect of profits derived from export of computer software, profits derived from export/transmission outside India of computer software or provision of technical services outside India in connection with development/production of computer software are exempt from tax up to a specified limit. Profits from export of computer software also include profits derived from on site development of computer software. Further, deduction under this section is also available to supporting software developers.

Deduction in Respect of Profits Derived from Export of Computer Software

Percentage of profits that can be claimed as a deduction under section 80HHE of the Act is as follows:

Financial year amount of deduction for the year 2001-02 – 70 per cent, 2002-03 – 50 per cent, 2003-04 – 30 per cent, 2004-05 onwards, no deduction.

Computer software for the purpose of claiming deduction under section 80HHE means a computer programme recorded on any disc, tape, perforated media or any other information storage device and includes any customized electronic data or any product/service of similar nature notified by the Board, which is transmitted from India to a place outside India by any means. The Central Board of Direct Taxes (CBDT) has notified a number of IT-enabled services (ITeS) such as back office operations, call centres, data processing, revenue accounting, payroll, medical transcription, insurance claim processing, content development and animation, website services, etc., in respect of which deduction under section 80HHE of the Act can be claimed.

Profits Derived from Export of Computer Software

Following undertakings are eligible to claim deduction in respect of profits derived from export of computer software under the provisions of sections 10A/10B of the Act:

Under section 10A undertaking, should have begun or should begin to manufacture computer software:

- on or after April 1, 1980, in any free trade zone;
- on or after April 1, 1993, in any electronic hardware technology park or a software technology park; and
- on or after April 1, 2000, in any special economic zone.

Almost 100 per cent of profits derived from export of computer software for a period of ten consecutive assessment years. However, deduction is restricted to 90 per cent of profits for assessment year 2003-04 and no deduction is available from assessment year 2010-11 onwards.

Under section 10A undertaking located in a special economic zone which begins to manufacture computer software on or after April 1, 2002, 100 per cent of profits derived from export of computer software for the first five consecutive assessment years and 50 per cent thereafter for next two assessment years. Further, under section 10B, export-oriented undertaking, 100 per cent of profits derived from export of computer software for a period of ten consecutive assessment years.

Existing units which commenced operations prior to April 1, 2000 and claimed deduction under the provisions of erstwhile sections 10A/10B, can continue to claim such deduction under the provisions of newly substituted sections 10A/10B for the unexpired period of ten consecutive assessment years.

Depreciation on Computers

As per the provisions of the Act, annual depreciation on computers can be claimed at the rate of 60 per cent of written down value at the beginning of the relevant financial year for income tax purposes. Therefore, under the written down value method, 84 per cent of cost of computers can be depreciated in the first two years.

Incentives for Venture Capital Fund (VCF) and Venture Capital Company (VCC)

A complete 'pass through' status has been provided to income distributed by a VCF/VCC from investments in a Venture Capital Undertaking (VCU). Accordingly, income received by a person out of investments made in a VCF/VCC shall be taxable in the hands of such person as if it were received from investments made directly in the VCU, while income of a

VCF/VCC will be exempt from tax under Section 10 (23FB) of the Act.

Beneficiary of Employee Stock Option Plan (ESOP)

Employee Stock Option Scheme (ESOS) to be taxed only at the time of sale as capital gains In the event ESOPs/ESOSs are in accordance with the guidelines issued by the Central Government, profits accruing to the employee on sale of shares/debentures/warrants allotted under the plan/scheme will be taxed only as capital gains. In cases where such shares/debentures/warrants are gifted by the employee, the transfer would be taxable as capital gains in the hands of the transferee, i.e., donee.

State Government Incentives and Concessions

Karnataka

The Karnataka government offers special assistance, incentives and concessions for the information technology industries which have investments in fixed assets upto Rs 100 crore. The explosive growth of information technology in Karnataka has been helped by the progressive policies of the government. In the Millennium Information Technology Policy, 2000 and the Millennium Biotech Policy, 2001, the following incentives and concessions are made available for the industries coming under information technology and bio-technology sectors.

Exemptions

1. Entry Tax
2. Purchase Tax*
3. Sales Tax*
4. Works Contract Tax*
5. Electricity Tax

* The sales tax, purchase tax, sales tax on fuel used for captive generation and works contract tax arising in construction of infrastructure facilities, have been discontinued but 4 per cent minimum floor rate is levied with effect from 2003.

Concessions

1. Rebate on the cost of land
2. Concession in stamp duty
3. Concession in registration charges
4. Concession in power tariff

Relaxations

1. Labour laws
2. Pollution control
3. Power supply
4. Zonal regulations
5. Floor area ratio

Supports Services

1. Single window clearances
2. Infrastructure support
3. Escort services
4. Incubation facilities
5. Venture capital

Entry Tax Exemption

Imposition of tax on entry of product from one state border to another is known as entry tax. This tax is levied in Karnataka for all kinds of products. However, information technology industries are exempted from payment of entry tax on computer hardware, computer peripherals and other capital goods including captive power generation sets, during implementation stage which can be extended up to five years from the date of commencement of implementations.

Concessions

Rebate on the Cost of land

Information technology/biotechnology units claiming rebate on the cost of land as per the Millennium Information Technology/Biotechnology Policy, shall initially pay the full cost of the land at the time of taking over the land/registration of lease cum sale deed, from the state agencies like KIADB, KSSIDC, KEONICS, K-BITS, etc. Once the industry is commissioned and creates employment as envisaged in the policy, the information technology/biotechnology unit can approach the K-BITS with appropriate documentary proof for claiming the concession. The K-BITS reimburse the amount of 15 per cent being rebate on the cost of the land allotted by the state agencies.

Exemption of Stamp Duty and Registration Charges

The tiny and small scale industries both in information technology and biotechnology sector taking up expansion, diversification and modernization, are also exempted from stamp duty. In the case of exemption of stamp duty for information technology and biotechnology companies who purchase land from the sources other than the state agencies, the company has to furnish a bank guarantee for an equal amount of concession stating that if the industry fails to generate the required number of employment within one year from the date of commercial operation, the government is at liberty to invoke the bank guarantee without any further notice. The revenue department (registering authority) gives the concession at the time of registration itself.

The stamp duty and registration charges have been reduced from 15.5 to 9.5 per cent further in view of rationalization in the structure of stamp duty, the exemption of stamp duty and registration charges has been withdrawn since April 1, 2003. In case the information technology/biotechnology unit concerned did not fulfil the prescribed conditions the K-BITS will recommend to the director for invoking the bank guarantee and adjust the amount to the government.

Exemption of Stamp Duty for Information Technology/ Biotechnology Parks

In the case of exemption of stamp duty for information technology/biotechnology parks the concerned developers/

company will have to approach the K-BITS along with all the necessary documents and furnish a bank guarantee for an equal amount of concession, for a period of four years. The K-BITS then examine the request and provide necessary secretariat services to the director information technology and biotechnology for issue of necessary certificate that the transfer of land for the establishment of information technology/ biotechnology park is eligible for availing 50 per cent exemption of stamp duty and registration charges and the revenue department (registering authority) gives concession at the time of registration itself. After three years from the date of registration of such land or on claiming of return of bank guarantee by the company concerned, the K-BITS will verify the fulfilment of the prescribed conditions. In case the company concerned fails to fulfil the conditions, specified for the world class standard park with a minimum built-up area within three years from the date of registration, the K-BITS recommends to the director, information technology and biotechnology for invoking the bank guarantee without any further notice and adjust the amount to government.

While issuing certificate for information technology/ biotech parks, the director information technology and biotechnology takes into consideration that an information technology/biotech park must be a park developed either by a real estate developer or by a company in any part of the state with world class facilities as specified below with a minimum built-up area of one lakh sq ft, in case of information technology park and 50,000 sq ft in case of biotech park.

The world class facilities as envisaged in the information technology/biotech policy to avail the concession offered will include the following:

- Uninterrupted power supply round the clock with generator backup.
- Uninterrupted water supply round the clock.
- Dedicated telecommunication and Internet connectivity.
- Round the clock security arrangements.

- Centrally air conditioned.
- Adequate fire fighting system.
- Adequate parking facilities.

It is also clarified that the 'first year' referred in the information technology/biotech policy shall be reckoned from the date of first sale/invoice.

Power Tariff Concessions

Software industries are treated as industrial (and not commercial) consumers and electricity tariff applicable to the industrial consumers is levied on such industries. Software industries, which need electrical power up to 5 KVA, are permitted to be established without any local restrictions and are made eligible for all incentives and concessions. However, with effect from September 1, 2003 the Karnataka Power Transmission Company Limited has changed its policy temporarily and information technology units are now treated as commercial units which will have to pay tariff at commercial rates.

As continuous uninterrupted and quality power supply is one of the prime requirements of sustenance and growth of information technology industries, these industries are given priority in the sanctioning and servicing of power. The information technology industries are also to be exempt from power-cuts without any time limit. Captive power generation sets installed by the information technology industry are eligible for the following incentive: Total exemption from payment of electricity tax without any time limit.

Relaxations

(a) *Labour Laws*: Simplified labour laws are applicable to information technology units. Karnataka Shops and Commercial Establishment Act 1962, Industrial Employment (Standing Order) Act 1946 and Industrial Dispute Act 1947 are to be relaxed for these industries.

(b) *Pollution Control*: Karnataka State Pollution Control Board has simplified the procedure for seeking clearances under the Air Act and the Water Act for the software companies that use captive DG sets.

(c) *Zonal Regulations*: Entrepreneurs are permitted to establish information technology units without locational restrictions either in industrial, residential or commercial areas.

(d) *Floor Area Ratio*: 50 per cent relaxation of the existing FAR allowed.

Supports Services

Single window clearance and escort services are provided at K-BITS for a quick clearance of the proposals for establishment of information technology units. There is also establishment of incubation centres primarily with private initiatives with complete start-up facilities in ten districts; further the state has promoted the venture capital fund called Karnataka Information Technology Venture Capital (KITVEN)

Concession for Mega Projects on Information Technology/ Biotechnology

Mega projects in information technology which invests more than 100 crore or that employs more than one thousand employees in the state of Karnataka. Similarly, mega project in biotechnology, which will have investment of more than Rs 50 crore or which will provide employment to 250 in Bangalore or 100 in other cities, in the state of Karnataka. This parameter is applicable to new company/units as well as in the expansion of an existing company.

The duration of investment or for creating employment in mega projects shall be two years from the date of commencement of commercial production. In case of mega projects, a unique package of concessions is worked out with respect to the needs of the company in addition to those stated in the policies. The mega projects under both the sectors get exemption of stamp duty and registration charges and other fiscal incentives as per the package of concessions envisaged in the respective policies. However, if the high level committee recommends for incentives/concessions over and above the package given in the information technology/biotech policies, such concessions need the approval of cabinet with the concurrence of the concerned departments and finance department.

Andhra Pradesh

In order to attract the maximum employment potential of the industry in the state and keeping in view the intensely cost-competitive nature of information technology sector globally, an employment-linked incentive has been introduced by the government of Andhra Pradesh. Following are the measures adopted:

(1) Exemption from environmental clearance;
(2) Exemption from zoning regulations for purposes of location;
(3) Fiscal incentives;
(4) Power tariff at rates applicable to industry;
(5) Exemption from sales tax;
(6) Self-certification for purposes of compliance of the following Acts:
   - Water and Air Pollution Act
   - Factories Act
   - Employment Exchange (Notification of Vacancies Act)
   - Payment of Wages Act
   - Minimum Wages Act
   - Contract Labour (Regulation and Abolition) Act
   - Workmen Compensation Act
   - Andhra Pradesh Shops and Establishments Act
(7) General permission to run a three-shift operation;
(8) Rebate in land cost keeping in view the high employment potential;
(9) Relaxation of FAR for information technology park; and

(10) Exemption from stamp duty, transfer of property and registration charges for all information technology parks, etc.

Detail explanation of the above measures of government is as follows:

Software industry is exempted from the purview of the Andhra Pradesh Pollution Control Act, except in respect of power generation sets. Industrial power tariff and all other admissible incentives and concessions applicable to industries in respect of power shall be applicable to the information technology industry, including those in the urban areas and 25 per cent concessional power tariff is allowed to the new information technology industrial units for a period of three years from the date of release of power or of going into actual commercial production whichever is earlier. The government has totally exempted, computer software from the payment of sales tax payable under the provisions of A.P. General Sales Tax Act, 1957. Information technology software industry is exempted from zoning regulations for purposes of location. Government agreed in principle to self-certification/exemption as far as possible for the information technology software industry from the provisions of the following Acts:

- Factories Act
- Employment Exchange (Notification of Vacancies) Act
- Payment of Wages Act
- Minimum Wages Act
- Contract Labour (Regulation and Abolition) Act
- Workmen Compensation Act
- Andhra Pradesh Shops and Establishments Act
- Employees State Insurance Act

General permission is accorded to run a three-shift operation to the information technology software industry.

Rebate in the cost of land allotted to an information technology industry by the state government is subject to the following conditions:

(a) The rebate is restricted to Rs 20,000 per job created or the cost of the bare land (excluding development charges/cost) whichever is less, subject to a ceiling computed at the rate 0.30 acre for every 100 jobs created (e.g., if 3,250 jobs are created the limit for allotment of land at concessional price would be 9.75 acre).

(b) The minimum number of employees to be hired by a company in order to avail the concession on land cost is 100 (corresponding to a ceiling of 0.30 acre of land).

(c) The minimum gross salary/wage for an employment to be considered to have been created would be Rs 5,000 per month.

(d) The period for which such employment would have to be sustained to be eligible to be reckoned for this incentive is two years.

(e) The number of employees to be considered for the purpose of this provision should not exceed the number arrived at by the formula: [no. of computer work stations at a location x (1.33) x number of shifts (of 8 hours each) operated by the company at the location].

(f) Andhra Pradesh Industrial Infrastructure Corporation (APIIC) specifies suitable guidelines to ensure that the benefit of this provision reaches a company only after it meets the stipulated conditions regarding job creation and that the employment figures reported are corroborated by other supporting data such as investment, turnover, returns filed with RBI, returns filed with STPI, Hyderabad, etc.

(g) Cost of these incentives to APIIC offsets against cost of government lands alienated to APIIC.

The concessions linked to employment generation is limited to the extent of the number of persons of Andhra Pradesh origin, employed by the company. A company will be free to employ persons as per their own policies subject to conformity with local regulations as applicable. However, the concessions available under this incentive will be restricted to the number of persons of Andhra Pradesh origin employed by the company. For the purposes of this provision, a person of Andhra Pradesh origin is defined as a person who, at the time of employment by the company has been a resident of the state of Andhra Pradesh; domiciled in the state of Andhra Pradesh; born in the state of Andhra Pradesh; studied in a school/college/university in the state of Andhra Pradesh; or a person either of whose parents were born or attended school/college/university in Andhra Pradesh or vere domiciled in Andhra Pradesh.

For information technology infrastructure companies establishing facilities on private/APIIC/government lands, concessions was in the form of rebate on registration and transfer of property charges and exemption from stamp duty on a tapering scale for sale/lease of built-up space to the information technology industry:

(i) for facilities established and sold/leased before 1-4-2000, 90 per cent rebate;

(ii) for facilities established and sold/leased on or after 1-4-2000 but before 1-4-2001, 70 per cent rebate; and

(iii) for facilities established and sold/leased on or after 1-4-2001 and up to 31-3-2002, 50 per cent rebate.

The other conditions were:

(a) This concession was available only to information technology parks notified by the Department of Information Technology and Communications and which provide certain minimum facilities like uninterrupted/backup power, reliable telecom links, etc.

(b) The rebate was applicable on the combined levy of registration fee, stamp duty and transfer of property duty and no total exemption of stamp duty is to be extended.

(c) This concession was available only for the first transaction, when the first sale by the infrastructure company is made to an information technology industry.

(d) The concession was available on the purchase of land by an information technology industry, establishing an information technology park for its own use, provided it does not avail the concession as mentioned, i.e. rebate on cost of land linked to employment.

For information technology industry/information technology infrastructure companies establishing facilities on private lands outside the limits of the Municipal Corporations and the nine surrounding municipalities of Hyderabad and Gaddiannaram village, relaxation of Floor Area Ratio (FAR) to the extent of 50 per cent of the prevailing norm was available. For example, if the normal FAR was 1.5, the FAR allowed in such cases was 2.25.

(h) This concession is available only to information technology parks notified by the Department of Information Technology and Communications and which provide certain minimum facilities like uninterrupted/backup power, reliable telecom links, etc.

(i) This incentive is not available in respect of government/APIIC lands allotted at a concessional price.

District headquarters and other major economic nodels in the state like Vijayawada and Tirupathi offer highly competitive locations for information technology parks for IT-enabled services as skilled and semi-skilled manpower is readily available at these locations and the cost of living is very low.

Investment Subsidy for New Information Technology (Hardware and Software) Industries

Investment subsidy is given on the basis of 20 per cent of the fixed capital investment but not exceeding Rs 20 lakh. However, in respect of entrepreneurs belonging to Scheduled Caste and Scheduled Tribe categories, the investment shall be 25 per cent of fixed capital cost, not exceeding Rs 50 lakh. This subsidy is not available to information technology industries availing of the rebate on land cost. Fixed capital investment, always mean the original fixed capital invested in the project before depreciation.

Special Incentives for Mega Projects/Pioneering Project

For mega projects, with investment exceeding Rs 100 crore, the government considers special package of incentives, on a case to case basis, based on the gestation period, pioneer nature of projects, vocational aspects, state of the art technology, profitability, scope for further related investments, etc. The package of concessions are initially valid for a period of three years and subject to review thereafter.

Maharashtra

Maharashtra is well developed in overall development of industries in the country during post reform period. Information technology is an important thrust area that is why the Government of Maharashtra celebrated 20th August, 2003 as Information Technology Day and announced a very progressive Information Technology and Information Technology Enabled Service Policy, 2003 with unique of features that establishes it as the information technology hub of India. Recent policy has announced several concessions, exemptions and relaxations. Relaxation is given for working hours, work shifts and employment of women under Shops and Establishments Act.

Other relaxations are made under the Industrial Disputes Act and Contract Labour Act to all information technology and IT-enabled service units in the state on par with Special Economic Zones (SEZs). Issuing special passes to vehicles transporting women workers of information technology and IT-enabled service units during night times is permitted. Further, information technology and IT-enabled service units are declared as public utility services and essential services. Information technology and IT-enabled service units are exempted from clearances of Maharashtra Pollution Control Board, and also suitably amended various labour laws for facilitating submission of reports/returns in electronic formats. Permission to information technology and IT-enabled service units for self-certification of reports and returns is given.

Fiscal Incentives

There is 100 per cent exemption of stamp duty to all information technology and IT-enabled service units in public information technology parks and units in 'C' 'D', 'D+' and 'No Industry District' areas, and 90 per cent exemption in stamp duty payment for mergers, de-mergers and reconstruction of information technology and IT-enabled service units all over the state. However, there is 75 per cent exemption in stamp duty if they are in private information technology parks. Stamp duty exemption is also available to non-information technology entities such as leasing and financial institutions acquiring space/premises in private and public information technology parks for subsequent leasing to information technology and IT-enabled service units. However, charging of sales tax at minimum floor rate of 4 per cent on all products of information technology and IT-enabled service is permitted and there is a simplification of procedures pertaining to 'F' and 'C' forms.

Support by Urban Local Bodies

Information Technology Policy, 2003 enables the government of Maharashtra to direct all municipal corporations to exempt from levy of octroi or tax on entry of imported capital and raw materials for information technology and IT-enabled service units. The levying of property tax on all establishments/buildings of them is to be on par with residential premises.

Further, all information technology and IT-enabled service units are granted 100 per cent additional floor space by paying certain premium both in public information technology parks and private information technology parks of specified sizes.

There is also a policy direction to municipal corporations/councils for a single window interface for all clearances/approval/licences required by information technology and IT-enabled service units. They are allowed to file self-certified reports/returns to the concerned officers.

Since information technology and IT-enabled service units do not cause any pollution, they are exempted from the requirement of No Objection Certificate (NOC) from Maharashtra Pollution Control Board (MPCB). In case exceptional situations arise in future, a negative list of such exceptional cases will emerge.

Relaxation with respect to labelling of items/products of information technology and IT-enabled service units under the Weights and Measures Act is permitted.

When an information technology/information technology enabled service unit effects a transfer of assets related to information technology and IT-enabled service from one branch to another, filling up of 'F' form is compulsory. The policy enables the government to get this requirement deleted with consent of the Government of India and also to simplify the working procedure in this regard.

Submission of 'C' form is compulsory for units in the state while buying transactions. Banks, information technology and IT-enabled service firms are not in a position to submit 'C' form and hence they are required to pay higher rate of sales tax. The policy enables the government to get this procedure simplified, with the consent of the Government of India.

Presently, 14 per cent Contract Tax is being charged on annual maintenance agreements for information technology products. Since proportion of spare parts required for maintenance of such products is very small, a maximum of 5 per cent works contract tax on annual maintenance agreements of information technology and IT-enabled service units are charged in the State.

Tamil Nadu

Unlike Karnataka and Andhra Pradesh, there is no system of Entry Tax or Purchase Tax in Tamil Nadu. Information technology industry is continue to enjoy facilities of unrestricted movement of capital equipment including hardware, peripherals, captive power gen sets, UPS sets and telephone exchanges, subject only to sales tax payments as per orders in force. Due to self-sufficiency in power, Tamil Nadu does not have power cuts for industry. The facility of uninterrupted power is continued to be offered to information technology industry.

Tamil Nadu has announced fiscal and tax concessions for investments of various slabs starting from an investment of Rs 50 crore (mega projects) upto investments exceeding Rs 1,500 crore (super mega projects) is applicable for information technology industries also in addition to other incentives. Capital subsidy as applicable to electronics industries at 20 per cent of fixed assets subject to a maximum of Rs 20 lakh will be available for all information technology industries, irrespective of their location in the state. Where the unit is also eligible for capital subsidy for backward/most backward areas, this special subsidy will become part of such subsidy. The existing incentives available for industries employing at least 30 per cent of women workers are also available to information technology industries.

Concessions/Incentives Available for IT Industries

Special Subsidy for Mega Projects

An industry set up anywhere in Tamil Nadu having an investment of Rs 50 crore to Rs 100 crore is eligible to a capital subsidy of Rs 25 lakh, Rs 100 crore to Rs 200 crore is eligible for a subsidy of Rs 50 lakh and Rs 200 crore and above is eligible for a subsidy of Rs 100 lakh.

Special Concessions for Super Mega Projects

(1) They are eligible for sales tax deferral/waiver for 14 years. The company can exercise its option either to avail deferral/waiver.
(2) The limit of only one revision of the eligibility certificate is applicable to super mega projects. They are permitted a maximum of five times of revisions of the eligibility certificate. The eligibility certificate indicates the investment made in fixed assets up to the date of its issue and represents the eligibility limit for availing sales tax deferral/waiver at any point of time. Once the investment limit and time limit for making the investment as specified for super mega projects are reached, the company is eligible for the concessions.
(3) These companies can continue to avail sales deferral/waiver upto the specified period of 14 years – even if the quantum of sales tax deferral/waiver availed reaches the limit of 100 per cent of the value of investment in fixed assets for the super mega projects before 14 years.
(4) If the quantum of sales tax deferral/waiver availed by these companies does not reach the limit of 100 per cent of the

investment in fixed assets for the super mega projects by the end of the 14th year, they can continue to avail sales tax deferral/waiver for a further period not exceeding seven years or till the limit of 100 per cent of the value of the investment in fixed assets for the super mega project is reached, whichever is earlier.

(5) The deferred sales tax is repayable in five equal annual instalments as follows:
- sales tax deferred in year one will be repayable in five equal annual instalments from year 15 to year 19;
- sales tax deferred in year two will be repayable in five equal annual instalments from year 16 to year 20 and so on;
- the deferred amount repayable in any particular year is to be paid in four equal quarterly instalments before the last day of each quarter.

Existing industries taking up expansion/diversification, at their existing plant location/sites or at new sites, for which investment in fixed assets exceeds Rs 1,500 crore (excluding the investment already made) within a time-frame of five years (relaxable up to seven years in special cases), is eligible for the concessions provided, they satisfy the additional turnover norms for expansion/diversification.

Additional Subsidy for Employing Women Workers

New industrial units (small, medium or major) where more than 30 per cent of the total workers employed are women shall be eligible for an additional capital subsidy of 5 per cent of investment in fixed assets subject to a ceiling of Rs 5 lakh.

Special Subsidy for Electronics Industry

Electronic units set up anywhere in Tamil Nadu are eligible for special subsidy of 20 per cent on fixed assets subject to a maximum of Rs 20 lakh.

Laws and Regulations in Information Technology Industries

Traditional regulation and competition policies have little role in the evolution and development of information technology industries. Economists neglect the vast consumer side economies, and their interactions with the more understood scale and scope factors on the production side, which drive firms to large size and dominance. Similarly, traditional anti-trust laws still hold on to the idea of an absolute value of a product to the consumer and of consumer independence.

These would mean an inability to recognize the functionality of a growing large firm giving great value to consumers. Traditional regulation or policy would also not be alert to the ways by which large dominant firms abuse their special position. The dominant firm in keeping itself in dominance could act to keep the industry at lower rates of innovations, lower levels of services and features. This need not take place in a manner that is obvious or recognizable. Such a dominant firm could lay the side possible superior ideas and innovations, which would therefore die, especially since their value is contingent upon the particular path chosen, and dominance can greatly influence that choice (Morris, 2003).

The problem is one of fundamental uncertainty and 'humps' in the evolution of information technology industries greatly reduce the value of prior expertize or experience as a guide. Furthermore, there is a basic difference between the information technology sector and earlier industries that amounts to making information technology industries fundamentally different from all others.

The arrival of the Internet and the world wide web made it possible for people to communicate and transact over cyber space. It was a revolutionary step for humanity, but it also created a significant need for the regulation and governance of these activities – a requirement that lead to the creation and implementation of cyber laws across the globe. India became the 12th nation in the world to adopt a cyber law regime during 2000.

Internet is a mode of communication. When civilization started, communication was through gestures; then speech was invented by human race. After many centuries, another simplified mode that came was writing. With the evolution of human races, man thought of easier and fast reachable mode of communication. Then came evolution of Internet; with this mode of communication, there was one language to speak throughout the globe.

To put in common man's language, Internet is a global network of computers; all of them speak same language. The real power of Internet is that it is available to anyone with a computer and a telephone. As Internet is proliferating like a web throughout the globe, so will the complexity of the cyber laws – many countries have already laid down cyber laws, India is proud to be one of them.

The Internet as with all path-breaking technological developments gives us all the opportunity to act as a global community, advertise and operate across all frontiers, over borders and beyond the control of any national government. Traditional legal systems have had great difficulty in keeping pace with the rapid growth of the Internet and its impact throughout the world. While some laws and objectives have been enacted and a few cases have been decided that affects the Internet, they leave most of the difficult legal issues to the future.

Information Technology Act, 2000

In India, cyber laws are contained in the Information Technology Act, 2000. The main objective of the Act is to provide legal recognition for transaction carried out by means of electronic data interchange and other means of electronic communication, commonly referred to as e-commerce, which involve the use of alternatives to paper-based methods of communication and storage of information, to facilitate electronic filing of documents with the government agencies. The Act aims to provide the legal infrastructure for e-commerce in India. At this juncture, it is relevant to understand what the Information Technology Act, 2000 offers and its various perspectives.

Exemptions/Exclusions

The Act shall not apply to the following categories of transaction:

(a) any negotiable instrument;
(b) a power of attorney;
(c) the trust;
(d) a will including any other testamentary disposition;
(e) any contract for the sale or conveyance of immovable property; and
(f) any other documents or transaction as may be decided by the Central Government.

Digital Signature (Chapter II)

With the passing of the Act, any subscriber (i.e., a person in whose name the digital signature certificate is issued) may authenticate electronic record by affixing his digital signature. Electronic record means data record or data generated image or sound, store, received or send in an electronic form or micro film or computer generated microfiche.

Electronic Governance (Chapter III)

Where any law provides submission of information in writing or in the type written or printed form, from now onwards it will be sufficient compliance of law, if the same is sent in an electronic form. Further, if any statute provides for affixation of signature in any document, the same can be done by means of digital signature. Similarly, the filing of any form, application or any other documents with the government authorities and issue or grant of any license, permit, sanction or approval and any receipt acknowledging payment can be done by the government offices by means of electronic form. From now onwards retention of documents, records, or information as provided in any law, can be done by maintaining electronic records. Any rule, regulation, order, by-law or notification can be published in the official gazette or electronic gazette.

The Act, however, provides that no Ministry or Department of Central Government or the State Government or any authority established under any law can insist upon acceptance of document only in the form of electronic record.

Regulation of Certifying Authorities (Chapter IV)

The Central Government may appoint a controller of certifying authority who shall exercise supervision over the activities of certifying authorities. Certifying authority means a person who has been granted a license to issue a digital signature certificate. The controller of certifying authority shall have powers to lay down rules, regulations, duties, responsibilities and functions of the certifying authority issuing digital signature certificates. The certifying authority empowered to issue a digital signature certificate shall have to procure a licence from the controller of certifying authority to issue digital signature certificates. The controller of certifying authority has prescribed detailed rules and regulation in the Act, as to the application for license, suspension of licence and procedure for grant or rejection of license.

Digital Signature Certification (Chapter VII)

Any person may make an application to the certifying authority for issue of digital signature certificate. The certifying authority while issuing such certificate shall certify that it has complied with the provisions of the Act. The certifying authority has to ensure that the subscriber (i.e., a person in whose name the digital signature certificate is issued) holds the private key corresponding to the public key listed in the digital signature certificate and such public and private keys constitute a functioning key pair. The certifying authority has the power to suspend or revoke digital signature certificate.

Penalties and Adjudication (Chapter IX)

If any person without the permission of the owner, accesses the owner's computer, computer system or computer network or downloads copies or any extract or introduces any computer virus or damages computer, computer system or computer network data, etc., he shall be liable to pay damage by way of compensation not exceeding rupees one crore to the person so effected.

For the purpose of adjudication, the Central Government can appoint any officer, not below the rank of director in the Government of India or any equivalent officer of any State Government, to be an adjudicating officer. While trying out cases of this nature, shall consider the amount of gain of unfair advantage or the amount of loss the aforesaid provisions were not incorporated in the Information Technology Bill, 1999 and the same were suggested by the select Committee of Parliament.

The Cyber Regulations Appellate Tribunal (Chapter X)

Under the Act, the Central Government has the power to establish the Cyber Regulations Appellate Tribunal. The Tribunal shall have the power to entertain the cases of any person aggrieved by the order made by the controller of certifying authority or the adjudicating officer.

Offences (Chapter XI)

Tampering with computer source documents shall be punishable with imprisonment up to three years or fine up to Rs 2 lakh or with both. Similarly, hacking with computer system entails punishment with imprisonment up to three years or with fine up to Rs 2 lakh or both.

Miscellaneous

Under the Act, any police officer not below the rank of deputy superintendent of police or any other authorised officer of the Central or State Government, may enter in public place and search for arrest without warrant, any person who is reasonably suspected or having committed or committing or of being about to commit any offence under the Act. 'Public place' includes any hotel, shop or any other place intended for use or accessible to public. The Information Technology Act will go a long way in facilitating and regulating electronic commerce. It has provided a legal framework for smooth conduct of e-commerce. It has tackled the following legal issues associated with e-commerce: (i) requirement of a writing; (ii) requirement of a document; (iii) requirement of a signature; and (iv) requirement of legal recognition for electronic messages, records and documents to be admitted in evidence in a court of law.

However, the Act, has not addressed the following grey areas:

(i) protection for domain names;
(ii) infringement of copyrights laws;
(iii) jurisdiction aspect of electronic contracts (viz., jurisdiction of courts and tax authorities);
(iv) taxation of goods and services traded through e-commerce; and
(v) stamp duty aspect of electronic contracts.

Basic Steps in E-Commerce

Trade or business begins with marketing or advertising. It is the same in the realm of e-commerce. Business activities even if conducted via the Internet or any other mode of e-commerce, can be broadly divided into four basic steps:

- Advertisement
- Agreement to buy/sell
- Delivery
- Payment

Advertisement

Offer or Invitation to Make an Offer

Advertisement is normally the first step towards concluding a business transaction. More and more companies are advertising on the net. It provides a wide audience at a low cost. The advertisement can be either an offer or an invitation to make an offer. A contract is generally concluded when the party to whom the offer is made accepts an offer made by one party. Thus, if any advertisement over the web, whether it constitutes an offer or not depends on the facts of each case. The underlying test to distinguish the same is simple and commonsensical. If the advertisement merely requires acceptance and nothing else, then the advertisement is interpreted as an offer. If the advertiser requires any person to furnish only information, naturally, it is to be construed as invitation to make an offer. Thus, it is important to keep this in mind while designing the website or while advertising on the web.

Violation of Any Law

Generally, the advertisement should not violate the laws of the countries where it is published, which in the context of the Internet could mean the entire world. Sometimes, the nature of the product or service advertised may be illegal in certain jurisdictions (like gambling or pornography). Thus, an appropriate notice and/or disclaimer should be included on the website.

Agreement to Buy/Sell

In an electronic transaction, the following issues need to be addressed:

- Are online contracts binding?
- When and where is the contract concluded?

Are Online Contracts Binding?

The electronic cash payment (ECP) adds clarity to this issue and expressly specifies that offer and electronic records can make acceptance. The problem with an online contract arises from the question of how to enforce a contract that does not have a document backing it and how this contract is to be proved in court.

Requirement of 'Documents'

Contracts that are written and signed are more certain and therefore easier to enforce. This is due to the fact that a document lends some degree of authenticity as to the contract formation and facilitates easier enforcement of the same. Documents are also required for evidence purpose under section 64 of the Indian Evidence Act except in the cases specifically provided for. The contents of any document which have to be proved by the original of the document itself being produced in court, except in a few limited instances. If a computer printout or any information, which is visible on the screen of the computer, is included in the definition of document, the question arises as to what is an original with respect to computer printout, or information contained in a computer. With respect to information stored on computers, it is possible to alter information without it being found out, so to speak. If communications between the parties are in the computer form, both parties can alter the information without the other party becoming aware of such alteration. If one party has altered the information, then both parties have a different document. The question will arise as to which document is the original. Indian law does not resolve this issue.

The ECP seeks to resolve this issue by stating that where the law requires any record to be presented in original form, that requirement is satisfied by an electronic record if there exists reliable assurances as to the integrity of the record and where it is required that a record be presented, that record is capable of being displayed to the person to whom it is being presented.

Formation of Online Contracts

Under the Indian Contract Act 1872, the acceptance of a valid offer results in a valid contract. It is crucial to know when a contract is concluded online and whether any difference exists between contracts concluded by traditional modes, such as via post. Section 4 deals with the rule regarding completion of communication of acceptance. The communication of acceptance is complete as against the offeree, when it reaches the knowledge of the offeror. But, the Supreme Court has held that in the case of communication by oral means, by telex or by telephone, an acceptance is communicated only when it is actually received by the offeror. This question has to be addressed in the case of e-commerce, where more often than not, acceptance is made via e-mail or by pressing the 'Accept' or 'Buy' icons. The question that would arise is when has the acceptance been conveyed, i.e., is it:

(1) when the e-mail was sent; or
(2) when it was received by addressee; or
(3) when it reaches the 'host computer' which provides the e-mail facility to the addressee.

In Germany, judicial practice has established that a message sent by e-mail is deemed to be received when it reaches the host computer of the addressee (if the addressee has published the e-mail address on his visiting card or letterhead or otherwise makes it publicly known). In South Africa, when the acceptance is by way of post, the contract will be concluded at the time when, and at the place from where, the acceptance is posted. This is known as the 'expedition' theory. Where the acceptance is notified by means of fax or telegram, the contract is concluded at the time and place where the offeror learns of the acceptance. This is called the 'information theory'.

Electronic Payment Systems

Electronic payment systems considered very insecure since it is possible for third parties to obtain these details and misuse them. Visa and Master Cards have developed a system for online payment called Secure Electronic Transaction (SET).

Electronic Cash

Electronic cash is more secure and anonymous than credit cards when making payments for transactions. It is specially useful for small transactions.

Electronic Cash Payment Mechanism: Open Bank-issuer Model (International)

Anyone wishing to use electronic cash can purchase a certain number of units from member bank for a particular value in a local currency. He or she can then use it for making payments over the Internet. The receiver of electronic cash can either use it for making similar payments over the Internet or redeem it at any member bank for his country's own currency. As electronic cash is not a legal tender, till participation of all the players is doubtful (including buyers, sellers, banks, etc.).

Some businesses in the credit card industry are attempting to introduce stored value cards in India. Like cash, it leaves no audit trail, and offers both parties secrecy, as the transaction can be as anonymous as a cash deal. Each card carries a computer chip and has a particular amount stored in it. This amount partially or wholly can be transferred to another card. Banks are not involved in the chain of transactions except for the initial loading and the final unloading of funds into and out of the card. For this purpose, the Reserve Bank of India (RBI) would have to create a 'bullion card' which will have a huge amount, say, Rs 100 crore in it. Other banks can then draw their own sums from this card and then sell it at a commission to the ultimate consumers. The RBI has been approached for permission to launch the card. India should start thinking and debating on introducing electronic cash or something similar to it. If any party to the transaction is a foreign party, the Exchange Control Regulations will also come into picture.

Major Legal Issues in E-commerce

- Security
- Jurisdiction
- IPR
- Privacy
- Liability
- Uniform laws for electronic commerce
- Content regulation
- Taxation

Though all the above-mentioned issues are important, those pertaining to security, jurisdiction, IPR and privacy have been dealt with further:

Security

Security is the single biggest obstacle for the growth of e-commerce. There are basically two kinds of security problems according to a survey; teenage hacking accounts only for 7 per cent of reported violations, while infiltration by competitor account for 39 per cent of the violations. Under the Indian Telegraph Act, 1885, "if any person with intention to prevent or obstruct the transmission or delivery of any message, or to intercept or to acquaint himself with the contents of any message, or to commit mischief damages, removes tampers with or touches any battery, machinery, telegraph line, post or any other thing whatever, being part of or used in or about any telegraph or in the working thereof, he shall be punished with imprisonment for a term which may extend to three years or with fine or both". There is a possibility that any attempt of hacking could be punishable under this section.

Securing Electronic Transactions

One of most important conditions for e-commerce's survival is the ability to safeguard all electronic transactions. Unless an electronic transaction is secure it would be difficult to determine its authenticity. Also, users will be hesitant to send confidential information over the net. Existence of safeguard and an assurance that such transmissions are foolproof will go a long way toward boosting e-commerce. The most common way of protecting electronic transactions is through cryptography (i.e., encryption techniques). Cryptography uses sophisticated mathematical algorithms, particularly a technology known as 'asymmetric cryptography'. Cryptography can be differentiated between the following:

- Use of cryptography for confidentiality of a message; and
- Use of cryptography in digital signatures.

Any person would like his transaction to be confidential. This can be achieved through encryption and decryption techniques. In this case, an encryption process would code a message and the coded message would then be transmitted over the net. Thus, only users having capability to decrypt that coded message would have access to the content. For successful decryption, it is important that the decrypting technique is corresponding to that particular encrypting technique.

It is also important that the encryption process is secure enough, so that it cannot be easily cracked. The strength of the encryption depends on the key length used by the encryption software. As of today a key length up to 128-bits can be used. Encryption however, may hamper national security, as detection of espionage activities by government authorities becomes more difficult.

Encryption and decryption techniques involve the use of two kinds of keys, public keys and private keys, both of which are mathematically linked. One key is used for encryption and other corresponding key is used for decryption. Each user has a pair of keys, of which the private key is kept secret and the public key is open to all. Thus, if X wants to send a message to Y, X will encrypt the message with Y's public key and send it to Y. Only Y would be able to access the message.

Digital Signature

The basic purpose of signing any document/contract is:

(1) To authenticate the document; and
(2) To identify and bind the person who signs the document or contract (endorser).

Once a signature is laid on paper the endorser cannot later falsely state that he had not signed the document and consequently cannot repudiate the same. It is possible to accord the same legal treatment to a digital signature, if such signature can perform the same function as a conventional signature.

Status of Digital Signature under Indian Law

A controller who will be appointed by the Central Government will control certification authorities. The duty of the controller would be to license, certify, monitor and oversee the activities of certification authorities. Certificates issued by a foreign electronic signature that comply with laws of a foreign jurisdiction would be recognized in India, if the laws of such country and practices of foreign certification authorities have a level of reliability at least equivalent to that required in India.

Intellectual Property Rights (IPR) Trade Marks and Domain Names

One of the first issues to arise in relation to IPR due to cyberspace was with respect to domain names. A domain name is your identity in the electronic world, akin to a trademark and makes you and your products known to both the existing and potential customers. A domain name is a corporate identifier. It represents not only your name and address but also your good will. The problem began when unrelated parties started registering domain names of famous brand like McDonalds and MTV. Prima facie the main purpose was to get a free ride on the reputation of this well established brand. The right·brand owners had to fight and in some cases pay up to get back domain names.

Indian companies have also faced their share of domain name disputes. In one case, a Tata group company, Titan Industries, registered the trademark 'tanishq'. A cyber squatter hijacked the domain name tanishq.com. The Delhi High Court granted an injunction in favour of Titan Industries. The Delhi High Court recently passed an interim order in domain name for (yahooindia.com). The court held that the cases fell under the doctrine of passing off and not trademark infringement. Relying upon this doctrine, it noted that due to the nature of Internet use, the defendant's appropriation of the plaintiff's mark as a domain name was valid ground to bring such an action.

Further, considering the vastness of the Internet and availability to the general public, disclaimer cannot adequately remedy such appropriation. The court acknowledged that even though the word 'yahoo' was a dictionary word, it has achieved distinctiveness and is associated with the plaintiff company and hence is entitled to maximum protection. As a result, the court granted an interim injunction restraining the defendants from dealing in service or goods on the Internet or otherwise under the trademark/domain name (yahooindia.com), or any other trademark/domain name that is identical to or deceptively similar to the plaintiff's trademark 'yahoo', till the disposal of the suit.

Hyperlinks

Hyperlinks allow a link to different pages at the same or different websites. A cause of concern is the potential loss of advertisement viewership on websites. This may happen if the hyperlink bypasses the advertisement of the second site and directly points to the content in such site.

In a Scottish case, Shetland moved the court against a direct link to news articles within the online publication of Shetland Times by an Internet-based news agency (Edinburg, 1996). The Internet-based news services published news headlines on their website and gave hyperlinks to the articles published by *Shetland Times*. Thus, technically they were not violating any copyright material. The Internet-based Caching is used by Chips on a regular basis. It entails duplication of a popular site on an 'as it is basis' on the servers of the ISP. The advantage to the ISP would be that its bandwidth requirement would reduce, as now it does not have to go out of its network every time someone clicks the URL of that website. While the intention may be good, it still could be held as copying and may violate the copyright of the original website. It may also attract penalty, both civil and criminal under the law. The ISP licence or the ECP does not offer any respite to this effect. India may be required to enact copyright laws in line with the US's Digital Millennium Copyright Act so as to allow caching.

Privacy

With the advent of the Internet, it has become easy for anyone to gather, compile and exploit private information of individuals. What were scattered, unimportant, small bits of data has now become a potent large set of data that can be misused by companies or by antisocial elements. This has prompted many countries to come up with legislation on privacy.

International Privacy Initiatives

On 25 July 1995, the European Union (EU) announced the adoption of a directive on the protection of individuals' personal data and on the free movement of such data. The directive seeks to prevent abuse of personal data and lays down comprehensive rules, including an obligation to collect data only for specified, explicit and legitimate purpose, as well as to only hold data if it is relevant, accurate and up-to-date.

The directive requires all companies concluding business in the EU to meet certain minimum standards of data protection. And the company that does not meet these stringent standards faces sanctions.

Indian Law Relating to Privacy

Significantly, India does not have any specific law governing privacy. The courts in India have not yet had the opportunity to look at privacy issues relating to the Internet. Analogies to the Internet will, therefore, have to be drawn from cases that the court has actually dealt with. The Constitution of India does not patently grant the fundamental right to privacy. However, the courts have read the right to privacy into the other existing fundament rights: Freedom to Speech and Expression, under Article 19(1) (a) and Right to Life and Personal Liberty under Article 21. In India, the right to privacy is one of the UN-enumerated rights granted to the individual. Barring a few exceptions, the fundamental rights secured to the individual are limitation on state action.

They are not meant to protect persons against the conduct of private persons. It is to be noted that the constitutional guarantee of the right to privacy is valid only against the state and no constitutional remedy for violation of privacy lies against any individual. Further, common law also does not provide direction for invasion of privacy. It seeks to provide protection by the use of civil wrongs such as defamation and breach of confidence. However, with the advent of e-commerce, such common law seems manifestly unsuited to this environment.

Thus, the Information Technology Act raises several real issues which have been discussed below:

(1) It demonstrates a legislature deeply skeptical of the Internet, rooted in the conventions of the past, yet battling with the need for an information technology law in the present day circumstances; this straddling of the known and unknown has strange results. In its desperate need to bring in some security for activity on the net it relies heavily on the executive, little realising that it can result in violation of civil rights particularly in light of India's infamous emergency. The absolute control it attempts to achieve over certifying authorities is worrying for the same reason. Thus, the Act lacks balance.

(2) While it is stated in the preamble that the Act has been passed "to facilitate electronic filing of documents with government agencies". Reading the Act makes one to question about this government Act because, for the ordinary middle class tax payers getting digital signature under the Act involves far too much hassle, too little security and the threat. They could be under government surveillance without their knowledge.

(3) The issue of privacy is a serious one which the Act imposes unfavourably on individuals as its appendix reveals. Thus, the Information Technology Act, 2000 needs some reworking.

(4) The primary disadvantage of this system lies in the case of loss of key word. If the key can be securely transmitted, so can the message! There has to be some method of ensuring that encrypted messages can be recovered if the private key is lost – retaining the technology to do so makes it easy for hackers. Further, where there is large number of users who will have to access the system, the secret key cryptography is potential unsafe because the risk of key falling into wrong hands is greater.

Conclusion

The comparative study of the various concessions extended by different states reveals interesting facts. Each state has its own way of attracting the information technology giants to come and set up their units but at the same time they have to fulfil the local needs of the people. Fortunately, all these leading four states have no dearth of information technology skilled workers as these states have established 80 per cent of the information technology related colleges, which will continuously supply skilled workers.

In all these states, support services are commonly found. The 'single window' clearances for information technology units, infrastructure support and relaxations in various labour laws specially Shops and Commercial Establishment Act, Industrial Dispute Act and Employment Act are provided in all the states.

No doubt, there is a flexible working hours and better pay perks but the workers in information technology and information technology enabled service in future will have to face lots of problems.

These services are now declared as public utilities and brought under Essential Services Act. At any time these workers may be retrenched and not allowed for unionism. Further, the industry will also face the problem of changing jobs by employees frequently (known as labour attrition) leading to high cost of training the freshers always. At present, the attrition rate in Indian information technology sector is as high as 30 to 35 per cent.

There is different yardstick for rebate on cost of land in Andhra and Karnataka. An entrepreneur in Karnataka will have to pay first, full cost of the land; once it is established and has provided minimum number of employment then he has to claim 15 per cent of rebate from K-BITS. This seems to be cumbersome and no big industrialist is ready to go through all these ordeals. On the other hand in Andhra Pradesh, the rebate on cost of land is Rs 20,000 per job created, subject to as many as eight conditions. Further, the government insists that if they want to avail such concession/rebate they have to employ only the people of Andhra Pradesh origin. A long definition is given for 'person of Andhra Pradesh origin'. This indicates that rebate and concession is linked to sons of the soil theory.

Maharashtra and Karnataka have entry tax, and thus exempted the information technology units on its imposition. Tamil Nadu has no such tax. However, all the southern states have accepted minimum floor rate of 4 per cent sales tax. Regarding the Information Technology Act, 2000, some apprehensions have been raised by several writers. The privacy of the individual in the Internet era is at stake – there is a need for reworking in the regulations of the cyber law in India to protect the violation of the civil rights.

•

5

Information Technology and Growth at Sub-National Level

The regional dimensions of growth of the Indian economy are assuming increasing relevance in the context of the progressive diffusion of structural reforms at the sub-national level. The quality of growth is getting increasingly assessed in terms of durable improvement in the regional growth profiles in which the interface between public policies for accelerating development and standards of living is the greatest. Moreover, regional patterns of growth provide a gauge of the quality of public policies themselves and their impact on macro-economic welfare. The various facets of the growth experience of states in India are critical for developing an understanding of the sources of demand generation as well as changes in productivity and growth. The growth performance in the states is often the outcome of institutional and non-economic factors interacting with the initial conditions which encompass various aspects of human capital development. Varying degrees of reforms in different states have yielded wide variations in growth performance. In this context, it has been pointed out that the popular characterization of backward states such as Bihar, Madhya Pradesh (MP), Rajasthan and Uttar Pradesh (UP) as homogenous group of poor performers does not hold good in terms of recent economic performance (Ahluwalia, 2002). It has also been argued that reforms have unshackled a number of states like Andhra Pradesh (AP), Gujarat, Karnataka, Maharashtra and Tamil Nadu who could achieve their true economic potential in recent years (Bajpai, 2000). From a completely different paradigm, the faster growth in select states has been interpreted as the operation of some kind of unbalanced growth with differing rates of catching up. Their other issues are raised in the context of Indian regional development, viz., fiscal, infrastructure and human resources development (World Bank, 2000).

Sub-National Growth Profile

The state-wise profile of per capita State Domestic Product (SDP) drawn up for 15 major states (representing nearly 90 per cent of Indian population) exhibits significant variation. In 1980-81, there were only four states, viz., Maharashtra, Punjab, Gujarat, and Haryana whose per capita real SDPs (at 1980-81 prices) were higher than the all-India per capita real GDP. The trend remained more or less similar in 1990-91. In the 1990s, this group expanded to include Tamil Nadu. Relative ranking in terms of absolute SDP need to be evaluated against a comparison of growth rates. In terms of trend growth rate (Table 5.1) Karnataka, West Bengal, Maharashtra, Tamil Nadu, and Andhra Pradesh have done well in the 1990s.

The regional growth experience of the 1990s suggests that states pursuing reforms seemed to have experienced higher growth rates in recent years with some tendency towards convergence. At the same time, the regional growth experience is indicative of some kind of unbalanced and divergent growth. The analysis of regional distribution and growth of industries in India by M. H. Bala Subrahmanya (2004) has brought out many noteworthy issues. Among the states, Maharashtra was the most industrialized region in 1970-71 and it has maintained its industrial supremacy over a period 1997-98. Since then,

Table 5.1
Trend Growth Rate of Per Capita SDP in India

	1980-81 = 100		*1993-94 = 100*
States	*1981-82 to 1990-91*	*1981-82 to 1993-94*	*1993-94 to 1999-2000*
1	*2*	*3*	*4*
Karnataka	4.0	4.5	4.5
Gujarat	3.3	3.1	2.4
West Bengal	2.7	2.9	5.6
Kerala	4.3	3.7	3.5
Tamil Nadu	3.9	4.2	5.1
Orissa	3.2	3.7	5.8
Maharashtra	2.2	3.1	5.1
Andhra Pradesh	2.6	2.7	5.7
Punjab	3.4	3.2	3.7
Madhya Pradesh	2.0	2.0	4.6
Uttar Pradesh	4.0	3.6	2.5
Haryana	2.7	2.3	3.2
Bihar	2.4	1.7	2.0
Rajasthan	2.5	0.9	2.7
India	3.4	3.2	4.8

Notes: 1. Due to non-availability of data, the average growth rates reported under column 4 for Madhya Pradesh, Gujarat and Kerala are calculated over the period 1993-94 through 1998-99.
2. The trend growth rates are calculated from semi-logarithmic function.

Source: Directorates of Economics and Statistics of respective State Governments.

the industrial status of West Bengal has gradually eroded. This is strikingly evident in terms of number of factories, fixed capital investment, employment and gross value added. In terms of employment, Tamil Nadu, AP, and Karnataka emerged more prominent in 1990s and accounted for nearly one-third of the total industrial employment in 1997-98. In terms of investment, Gujarat has emerged as the second-most important state in the country in 1997-98. However, in terms of investment and employment, the status of Bihar declined considerably. Given this, it is possible that India might experience a concentrated industrial growth confined to the "eight leading states" in the immediate future (ibid.).

Information Technology and State Economies

In the world of hi-tech economy, how do the states perform? How do the policy of state governments vary? How is the proactive support of the bureaucrats in the new ICT revolution? These will be highlighted in this section. In the world of software development, one speaks of measuring oneself on Capability Maturity Model (CMM-Level). It has five levels the lower-most called 'Initials' is at level 1 and the highest called 'optimizing' is at the level 5.

On behalf of the Department of Information Technology, Government of India, NCAER made a survey in 2003 about the development and penetration of information technology in the State economies. It has revealed through a headline "E-Readiness: Leaders and Laggards". In this survey, states have been rated on five parameters, viz., network access, network learning, network society, network economy and e-governance. Further, states have been slotted into six categories as: (1) leaders, (2) aspiring leaders, (3) expectants, (4) average achievers, (5) under achievers, and (6) laggards.

Figure 5.1

States E-Readiness: The Leaders and the Laggards in the Information Technology in India

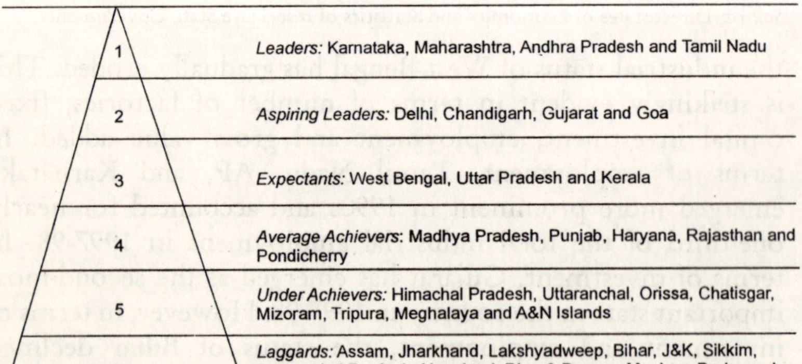

Highlights

(1) Karnataka, Andhra Pradesh, Tamil Nadu, and Maharashtra are the leaders in terms of 'e-readiness'.

(2) In terms of 'network access', Delhi has been rated as the best state, in view of high teledensity, percentage of household with phones and cable TV, cell phones, PC population, Internet connection, length of optical fibres in operation, and number of villages covered by village public telephones.

(3) In terms of 'network learning', five states: Chandigarh, Maharashtra, Delhi, Karnataka, and Tamil Nadu are on top. It is mentioned in terms of percentage of college and schools with Internet access and computer labs, universities offering information technology courses, number of websites of schools and colleges, etc.

(4) In terms of 'network society', Karnataka and Chandigarh are also ahead of others in maintaining these, which is measured on number of online companies, local language websites and interfaces, number of government websites, and of households having access of Internet with computers and phones.

(5) In terms of 'network policy', Maharashtra, Tamil Nadu, Chandigarh, Karnataka, Goa, and Gujarat are the best. This is evaluated on government's efforts to address issues related to telecom. E-commerce, taxation, IPR and presence of information technology policy and cyber laws.

(6) In terms of 'e-governance', Karnataka, AP, Tamil Nadu and Gujarat are on top that depends on the rural information technology applications in agriculture, education, medicine, trade-infrastructure initiatives and success related to e-governance projects like e-procurement, land registration, utility bills, etc.

(7) In terms of 'network economy', Maharashtra alone is on top. This is rated, based on numbers of information technology parks, floor area of information technology parks, sales turnover of information technology

companies in the states and number of jobs that require information technology skills.

Reasons for their Leading Role

In order to ascertain the leading role of first category four states in India, an in-depth study has been made into the real causes. The leading states have their own edge over other states in the following areas:

- Supply of information technology skilled workers;
- Infrastructure, specially bandwidth;
- Proactive policy environment; and
- E-governance.

Supply of Information Technology Skilled Workers

Huag's (1991) study in the US showed that five main factors play a part in the locational decisions of new software companies: (i) labour availability; (ii) infrastructure; (iii) quality of life; (iv) proximity to customers; and (v) previous employer and residence.

One of the reasons for a strong presence of ICT industries in the southern leading states in India is due to base created by establishing technical colleges, institutes and universities which provide required qualitative and truly world class engineers. In addition, with the revolution of electronics and communication, the knowledged workers in these states earn less than their counterpart in developed world, can have easily become part of the global economy. In order to correlate this view, the data on number of colleges/institutes and their intake have been culled from the AICTE data base. The results are truly encouraging and there is a strong correlation between the numbers of engineering graduates coming out from these states and the establishment of ICT firms in such states.

It is evident from the Table 5.2 that during 2000-01, total number of information technology related engineers (only diploma and graduates in electronics and communication science and MCA graduates) intake from 3,046 colleges are

1,63,630. Out of which 80 per cent are from four leading states such as Tamil Nadu, Karnataka, Maharashtra and Andhra Pradesh. In terms of number of institutes and intake in imparting Diploma/Degree/Master courses in information technology related courses, Tamil Nadu is having 717 institutes with 43,248 engineering seats intake capacity, followed by Maharashtra with 550 institutes but an intake of 32,598. AP has 544 institutes with 29,765 intake capacity.

Table 5.2

Statewise Engineering Colleges Sanctioned and Their Intake for Courses/Programmes in Computer Science/Information Technology during 2000-2001

States	*Diploma level*		*Degree level*		*MCA Level*		*Grand Total*			
	Institutes	*Intake*	*Institutes*	*Intake*	*Institutes*	*Intake*	*Institutes*	*%*	*Intake*	*%*
Tamil Nadu	161	8690	413	27263	143	7295	717	23.5	43248	26.4
Karnataka	320	8150	201	14185	69	3075	590	19.4	25410	15.8
Maharashtra	214	11005	317	20723	19	870	550	18.0	32598	19.9
Andhra Pradesh	106	5475	271	17695	167	6595	544	17.8	29765	18.5
Uttar Pradesh	79	2557	144	8568	44	2240	267	8.6	13365	7.8
Gujarat	50	2586	52	3190	10	480	112	3.6	6256	3.6
Kerala	42	1740	57	3368	7	210	106	4.0	5318	3.1
West Bengal	24	800	70	3820	10	355	104	3.4	4975	3.2
Delhi	19	895	12	710	7	310	38	1.2	1915	1.2
Goa	3	100.4	240	7	310	14	0.4	650	0.4	
Chandigarh	2	70	2	60	–	–	4	0.1	130	0.1
Total	1020	42068	1543	99822	4 83	21740	3046	100	163630	100

Source: Computed from:
1. Rajya Sabha unstarred question no. 1548, dated 9.3.2001.
2. Website: www.indiastat.com

Karnataka has more number of institutes (590) compared to Maharashtra and AP but intake capacity is 25,410. The rest of the 7 states constitute just 20 per cent of the total intake in India. It indicates that the presence of well established educational institutes lead to the upsurge in the knowledge economy of the leading states.

In terms of intake capacity in both diploma and degree level engineering colleges, Maharashtra takes the lead. On the other hand, intake at MCA and degree level engineering, it is Tamil Nadu which is leading. Thus, it is clear that undoubtedly in the southern four states along with Maharashtra the information technology education has played an important role in stimulating the state economies during the reform period.

The aspiring leaders in the information technology such as Delhi, Gujarat, Goa and Chandigarh can fulfil their desire to become leaders shortly, due to large number of e-learning activities. The problem is with those states which are called as Laggards. Where there is a need for establishing all kinds of network activities, in order to support both information technology use and production, states need to develop capabilities in the form of human resources with business skills. The most effective policies are those that promote use and production close to use and those have to have close consultation with private sector and academic institutions, and if the efforts of related government agencies is coordinated so that they complement, rather than compete with each other, the result can be a rapid diffusion of the technology, with broad benefits for the states.

Infrastructure, specially Bandwidth

The demands on the telecom infrastructure span an enormous range. While software firms, other exporters and multinationals require robust high bandwidth international links, the great majority of Indian states have little access to the most basic voice services. It may seem that the needs of this range of users are so different that they require very different solutions. This is partly true, but technological convergence, and the fact that the domestic and international networks must interconnect, imply benefits to integrated approaches to infrastructure improvements (Nirvikar Singh, 2003). We therefore examine the network at several states in terms of the number of STPI centres and bandwidth available to different leading states in the country. From the Table 5.3 it is evident that the bandwidth available to different states through STPI centres vary from state to state.

Table 5.3

Statewise Bandwidth Available at STPI Centres as on 2001

States	*Existing STPI centres (No.)*	*Proposed STPI centres*	*Bandwidth available (kbps)*	*% to the Total*
Tamil Nadu	2	4	7168	5.31
Maharashtra	2	3	15872	11.77
Karnataka	2	2	37184	27.57
Andhra Pradesh	2	3	28544	21.16
Uttar Pradesh	1	1	34496	25.58
Gujarat	1	1	10816	8.02
Kerala	1	1	768	0.56
West Bengal		1	–	–

Source: 1. Computed from the record of Lok Sabha Unstarred Question No. 4609, dated 19.12.2001.
2. www.indiastat.com

Karnataka is leading with 37,184 kbps bandwidth available, accounting for 27.57 per cent of the total bandwidth, followed by UP with 25.58 per cent and Andhra Pradesh 21.16 per cent and Maharashtra 11.77 per cent. The second highest bandwidth available to Uttar Pradesh is due to Noida STPI Centre which covers the firms from UP, Delhi and MP. It is an Export Process Zone under the control of the Central Ministry.

Andhra Pradesh is third in the list due to presence of large number of foreign companies next only to Karnataka. Thus, we can say that the performance of information technology in these states is doing better compared to other states due to presence of large amount of available bandwidth. In future, perhaps the growth of the state economy will be assessed not only by per capita SDP, but also by per capita bandwidth available.

Proactive Policy Environment

Since 1991 India has pursued polices of economic liberalization, but policy reform has been uneven. Controls on private industry and non-tariff trade barriers have been removed or substantially reduced, but liberalization has been slower in certain states where there is clear interest group opposition, such as labour laws and privatization. Reform has also been slow in those states where new regulatory institutions were needed to be created; there is still a substantial amount of learning by the doing that is taking place. Government revenue considerations also affect policy decisions in areas such as import tariffs and telecom privatization. The information technology sector in India is important not just because of its performance and potential, but because these factors have influenced the policy environment in India. The experience of different states exhibits a different picture. The states having the dynamics and IT savvy Chief Ministers have shown a tremendous growth of their economies. For instance, Karnataka has achieved 8 per cent growth rate as against 4.5 per cent of all-India growth rate in 2002-03, merely due to conducive policy of the state government and information technology savvy Chief Minister, S.M. Krishna. The conducive policy of the state paved the way for establishing the first software technology park of India in Bangalore, which provided the necessary infrastructure to reinforce the formidable skill advantages the region already possessed. Bangalore became central to the expansion plans of domestic firms, and the first choice within India for the large number of foreign companies from Silicon Valley (Rao, 1995). Therefore, Bangalore is truly called as Silicon Valley of India.

E-Governance

This is one area, where the government is providing indirect support for the information technology sector by boosting the domestic market through its own purchases. Of course, purchases of sophisticated equipment and software that sits unused in high-level bureaucrats' offices will have little positive impact. However, there are reasons to be more optimistic about the use of information technology in the government.

There are two broad uses of information technology for improved government functioning. First, back-office procedures can be made more efficient so that internal record-keeping, flows of information and tracking of decisions and performance can be improved. Second, when some basic information is stored in digital form, it provides the opportunity for easier access to that information by citizens. The simplest examples would be e-mailing requests or complaints, checking regulations on a web page, or printing out forms from the web so that a trip to pick up the forms from a physical office can be avoided. More complicated possibilities are checking actual records, such as landownership or transactions. Still more complicated are cases where information is submitted electronically by the citizen (Jagdish, 2003). What is encouraging is the number of examples of successful pilot e-governance programmes that have made some of the above actions possible.

These examples include:

- The 'Bhoomi project' of Karnataka, an e-governance project which computerized 20 million rural land records belonging to over 6.7 million farmers and delivering them through 177 government kiosks.
- It is a trendsetter for better governance and helped to eliminate red tapism and corruption in civic services.
- Computer-aided registration of land deeds and stamp duties in AP, reducing reliance on brokers and possibilities for corruption.
- Computerization of rural local government offices in AP for delivery of statutory certificates of identity and landholdings, substantially reducing delays.
- Computerized checkpoints for local entry taxes in Gujarat, with data automatically sent to a central database, reducing opportunities for local corruption.

- Consolidated bill payment sites in Kerala, allowing citizens to pay bills under 17 different categories in one place, from electricity to university fees.
- E-mail requests for repairs to basic rural infrastructure such as handpumps, reducing reliance on erratic visits of government functionaries.

While the extent of such programmes, and therefore, their benefits are still very limited, one of the essential characteristics of information is that it is a non-rival good. Hence, there is every reason to believe that the economics of such projects will continue to improve, particularly if costs of access continue to fall. It is important to note that once Internet access is available, its benefits are not restricted to e-governance. Individuals can obtain job information, advice on farming techniques, and so on.

In the field of e-governance the state of MP has done an excellent work through its 'Gyandoot' e-project even though it comes under 'average achievers' category. AP is at the level 2 called 'repeatable' level of maturity. Whereas the state of Karnataka is at level 1 that is level of initials (ibid.). Therefore, so-called leaders of information technology revolution are behind the average achievers so far as ICT to the masses is concerned. The detailed discussion about e-governance projects is made in the Chapter 6.

Contribution of Information Technology in the Leading States

Export of Software

The past decade has witnessed the rise of the Indian information technology sector from a position of virtual non-existence, to one, where it has occupied a place of pride in the global information technology industry. The Indian information technology sector has grown from a mere $ 6.4 billion in 1998-99 to $ 13.6 billion in 2001-02. The information technology industry today accounts for 2.87 per cent of India's

GDP. Exports from the Indian Software industry accounted for over half the industry's revenues, accounting for US$ 5.5 billion of the total information technology pie of US$ 10.5 billion in 2001.

The domestic market was dominated by hardware at US$ 2.9 billion, followed by services at US$ 1.6 billion, and packaged software brought up the rear with earnings of US$ 409 million. The information technology software and services export segment has a very crucial role to play in the overall information technology market in the country. The information technology software and services exports have greatly contributed to the information technology sector which enlarged from US$ 1.73 billion in 1994-95 to a US$ 13.5 billion industry in 2001-02 (NASSCOM, 2002).

Table 5.4

Regionwise Exports of Software and Electronic Hardware in India (2001-02)

($ million)

Region	*Software*	*Percentage to total*	*Hardware*	*Percentage to total*
Southern Region	4087	48.15	379	31.16
(a) Karnataka	2201	25.90	–	–
(b) Tamil Nadu	1231	14.50	–	–
(c) Andhra Pradesh	613	7.20	–	–
(d) Kerala	42	0.28	–	–
Northern Region	2316	27.28	334	27.46
(a) Uttar Pradesh	943	11.10	–	–
(b) Delhi	839	9.88	–	–
(c) Haryana	157	1.84	–	–
(d) Other States	377	4.44	–	–
Western Region	1869	22.01	488	40.13
Eastern Region	216	2.55	15	1.25
All India	8488	100	1216	100

Source: UNI data published in *Deccan Herald* 1-1-2003.
(–) not available

Among the various states, Table 5.4 reveals that southern region is leading in software export and services while western region is leading in hardware export. Within the southern region, Karnataka is leading with 25.90 per cent of the total exports in India followed by Tamil Nadu with 14.50 per cent. Similarly, in northern region, Uttar Pradesh is leading with 11.10 per cent of the total software export followed by Delhi with 9.88 per cent. In the western and eastern regions, there are no break-up figures available but it is Maharashtra in west and West Bengal in the east which are leading in exports.

Information Technology Enabled Services

The continued economic slowdown in a global market led to increase the use of outsourcing in the information technology sector and decreased the spending on new applications development and systems integration by several information technology companies in several states of India. Most of the companies focused almost exclusively on cost saving when making decisions to buy information technology services. The focus on financial services increased the role of chief executive officer in information technology services. The offshore services have grown at 20 per cent in 2003 for applications outsourcing services. The major Indian companies are Wipro, Infosys and Satyam located in Bangalore.

Some companies have struck allowances and partnership with Business Process Outsourcing (BPO) firms. The BPO is also growing at the rate of 25 per cent in 2003. Information technology enabled services are mostly in human resource (HR), finance, recruiting, shipping, distributing and logistics and indirect procurement. There is a virtual comparative advantage in terms of operating costs as well as salary costs in these activities of the companies. The possible areas of ITeS are:

ITeS – Possible Areas

Specialty Services	*Client Management*	*IT Management*	*HR and Benefits*	*Finance*
Tax planning	Call centre operations	Data centre management	Payroll processing	Fixed assets records
Regulatory	Customer satisfaction surveys	Network management	Recruitment	Project accounting
Transfer pricing	Order processing	Application development	Performance evaluation	A/P and A/R management
Facility management	Service support	Maintenance	Training administration	Reconciliation

The states which have the comparative advantages due to large pool manpower specially the South Indian states, with low cost of operation have succeeded in ITeS. It is forecasted that ITeS will grow by 15-fold over 2002-08 with a $21-24 million dollar amount. They (offshore vendors) will have about 40-50 per cent cost saving and vast availability of BPO market in the world, growing at the rate of 12 per cent per annum. The importance of ITeS is highlighted by NASSCOM, as is evident from the Table 5.5.

Table 5.5

Compound Annual Growth Rates of ITeS in Total Revenue Earnings in India from 1999-00 to 2003-2008E

(in million)

	1999-00	*2000-01*	*2001-02*	*2002-03E*	*2008E*	*CAGR 02-08(%)*
Software services	147,500	242,500	294,000	358,000	1,886,500	36
ITeS	24,000	41,000	71,000	117,000	1,102,500	58
Total (Rs)	171,500	283,500	365,000	475,000	2,989,000	42
ITeS % of total revenue	14	14	19	25	37	

Note: E – Expected.

Source:: Adapted from Sudheesh Venkatesh, paper presented at the IT Professionals Forum, 16 February, 2003, Bangalore.

NASSCOM has forecasted that India's revenue from ITeS during 2001-02 was Rs 7,100 crore and will grow Rs 8,100 crore by 2008. It has predicted that employment in the ITeS industry could rise to 1.1 million by 2008. It has also revealed that ITeS sector has emerged as a leading employment generator with 68,000 people already employed and additional 36,000 jobs will be created in the year 2002-03. The top five focus markets for ITeS companies include insurance, e-commerce, technology vendor, financial services and telecommunication services. Since the data at disaggregated level are not available, deliber ately the comparative study among the states is not done. However, it is presumed that again leading states are leaders even in their ITeS services due to large pool of skilled manpower available at cheaper rates.

Conclusion

In conclusion, investment in infrastructure, physical, capital and education is the key to economic development. This is, of course, an old policy prescription in the economics of development. What is new in the analyses is the view that the information technology content of these investments should be high. The use of information technology is so widely spread in the world economy, that no single country can ignore any longer the needs to invest in these technologies if it wants to improve the standard of living of its citizens (Pohjola, 2002). Following Pohjola's view we strongly feel that the use of information technology should be so widely spread in India that no single state can ignore any longer the needs to invest in these technologies if it wants to improve the standard of living of its citizens.

6

Importance of Information Technology Projects in E-Governance: Some Success Stories

E-governance is beyond the scope of e-government. While e-government is defined as a mere delivery of government services and information to the public using electronic means, e-governance allows direct participation of constituents in government activities. Blake Harris summarizes e-governance in this manner: "E-governance is not just about government website and e-mail. It is not just about service delivery over the Internet. It is not just about digital access to government information or electronic payments. It will change how citizens relate to governments as much as it changes how citizens relate to each other. It will bring forth new concepts of citizenship, both in terms of needs and responsibilities". E-governance will allow citizens to communicate with government, participate in the governments' policy making and citizens to communicate with each other. E-governance will truly allow citizens to participate in the government decision-making process, reflect their true needs and welfare by utilizing e-government as a tool. Introduction of e-governance is a key to make information technology relevant to ordinary citizens in India, where a large number of the population are poor and a digital divide is a significant problem. E-governance will allow ordinary people to constantly interface with the government in both local and central level on various matters. In this chapter successful e-governance projects in selected states of India are discussed. The selection is based on the most popular project in the state announced by respective state governments.

Accordingly, the following e-governance projects have been thoroughly discussed. They are:

- Bhoomi project in Karnataka
- E-Seva project in Andhra Pradesh
- Gyandoot project in Madhya Pradesh
- Warana Wired Village (WWV) project in Maharashtra
- Sustainable Access in Rural India (SARI) project in Tamil Nadu

India can look at becoming an information and knowledge society if it can bridge the existing digital divide and reach down to the grassroots levels. "E-goyernance is stated to be Rs 1,400 crore market, which has grown at 18 per cent in 2001-02, could also become instrumental in kick-starting the domestic usage of information technology in India. This can happen provided the government makes e-governance a part of administration and ensures that at least three per cent of its budgets are committed to information technology. It would also require measures to change the present information technology spending (NASSCOM, 2003). In light of this, the performance of leading states in e-governance is analyzed by taking one successful project in each state.

E-Governance Project in Karnataka

There is no denying that Karnataka has had the privilege of being the *numero uno* as far as information technology business and information technology resources are concerned. The current government has also been quite proactive in encouraging and supporting this industry. It has gone further by recognizing the role of biotechnology and ensured Karnataka's presence in the field of hi-tech knowledge based domains. With this kind of credentials, it is natural for people to expect the government to leverage information technology in the management of the state. The government also, perhaps, believes so and, from time to time has been announcing its achievements.

Mahiti: Millennium Information Technology Policy

Karnataka is the first state to announce information technology Policy in the year 1997. This policy has acted as an important catalyst for the growth of information technology industry in the state. The information technology usage is becoming more widespread and relevant.

Bhoomi: Online Delivery of Land Titles in Karnataka

Land record is a crucial document in the lives of people. It is essential for security of loan tenures, crop loans, bail applications, getting scholarships for children, planning rural development programmes, etc.

In Karnataka, 20 million land records containing details such as ownership, crop, bank loans, irrigation, etc., covering 67 lakh farmers spread over 27,000 villages, were kept in manual format. Nearly 9,000 village accountants were the lords and masters of these data. As a result, the system was plagued with corruption, like tampering of documents, non-availability of records in time, non-updation of records and non-availability of instant data for planning purposes.

Problems of Manual System of Land Records

The manual system of land records maintenance was highly opaque. Nearly 200 lakh records were maintained. The sub-district office did not have any updated copy of such records. Thus a situation of virtual monopoly of village accountants over these records was prevailing for many years. Records were not open to public scrutiny and were updated many a times only on various considerations.

Prone to Manipulations

Manual record administration was prone to manipulation. There have been large instances of government land being shown in the name of private parties. In fact, in Bangalore division alone 25 billion worth of government land had been manipulated and shown in the name of private influential persons. Opaque manual system facilitates such manipulation very easily by unscrupulous officials.

Harassment and Extortion

Many a times farmers faced harassment and extortion for not only provision of land records to them by the village officials but also for processing requests for change in land title.

Delay in Delivery of Land Records

On many occasions such delay was unintentional. Even if a village accountant was willing to give such records in time, he was not available when farmers wanted him most, as he was manning more than 4-5 villages. Therefore, there was no certainty about timely availability of such records when a farmer required them.

Cumbersome Mutation Process

The process of mutation (change in land title) was very cumbersome. Applications were being given to village officials who virtually enjoyed discretion of either processing them or not. As records were maintained in decentralized manner, there was no reporting mechanism available at sub-district level about the pendency of such applications with village accountants. Lack of any monitoring mechanism in manual system made farmers amenable to all pressures from hierarchy of the Department.

Lack of Timely Data for Planning Purpose

Land records contain various useful data like soil type, irrigation details, trees, crops grown, crop yield, etc. All such data is very valuable for various administrative purposes. As data was manually maintained, it was not possible to collate and analyze such data resulting into a mine of such useful data not being used in any meaningful way.

Cumbersome Crop Loan Mechanism

Banks often asked various land records before lending crop loans to farmers. Farmers in turn had to hunt village officials with no guarantee that banks would not ask for any more records. This made crop loaning process prone to delay and resulted in harassment to farmers.

Delay in Disposal of Civil Litigations

The courts often required various land records for disposing land based civil litigations (which formed more than 70 per cent of total litigations). Records were not forthcoming from village accountants easily and in time resulting into delay in disposal of civil litigations. Farmers had to often spend, in many cases more than 5-10 years, for disposal of their land litigation cases in absence of these records. Two types of records were maintained in revenue department: (1) registers, which indicated the current ownership of each piece of land, its area and cropping pattern, and (2) village maps that reflected the boundaries of each piece. Requests to alter land records (upon sale or inheritance of a land parcel) had to be filed with the village accountant. However, for various reasons the village accountant could afford to ignore these 'mutation' requests. Upon receiving a request, the village accountant is required to issue notices to the interested parties and also paste the notice at the village office. Often, neither of these actions was carried out, and no record of the notices was maintained. Notices were rarely sent through post. An update to the land records was to be carried out by a revenue inspector, if no objections were received within a 30-day period. In practice, however, it could take 1-2 years for the records to be updated. Landowners find it difficult to access the village accountant, as his duties entail traveling. The time taken by village accountants to provide the record of Rights, Tenancy and Crop Inspection (RTC) has ranged from 3 to 30 days depending upon the importance of the record for the farmer and the size of the bribe. A typical bribe for a certificate could range from Rs 100 to Rs 2,000. Land records in the custody of village accountant were not open for public scrutiny.

Even where accountants were law-abiding, village maps could not remain accurate as land was parcelled out into very small lots over generations. The system of physical verification of records by deputy tehsildars (supervisors of village accountants) became weak as the number of records multiplied and these functionaries were burdened with a host of other regulatory and developmental work.

Highlights of Bhoomi E-Governance Project

- Fully online system to carry out mutations on land records data.
- Finger print biometrics authentication to ensure fool-proof authentication system and to enforce the concept of non-repudiation.
- Facility to scan the field mutation order passed by revenue authorities and the notice served on the public.
- Land record centre in each 'taluk' office for public interface.
- Syncronizes with the regular field work done by village accountants and revenue inspector.
- Provision for interfacing of touch-screen kiosk at taluk office.

The above features have helped in bringing total transparency in land records administration with added advantage of security and reliability. The Bhoomi project changed the entire system by compressing the entire data into digital format and setting up touch-screen kiosks. A computerized land record kiosk (Bhoomi Centre) is operational in all of the 177 taluks in

Karnataka. Copies can be obtained for any land parcel in the taluk by providing the name of the owner or the plot number.

A village accountant is available full-time at these kiosks. When a change of ownership takes place through sale or inheritance, farmers can file for a mutation of the land record at the Bhoomi centre. Each request is assigned a number by the computer. The number can be used to check the status of the application on a touch screen provided on a pilot basis in three of the computerized kiosks. The computer automatically generates notices, which are then handed over to the village accountants. Most village accountants are not stationed at taluk offices, but they visit the central taluk office every 2-3 days to pick these papers.

The process of issuing notices by village accountants to the interested parties remains the same. And as before, the revenue inspector who is stationed in the field, approves changes to the land record 30 days after the notices are served, provided that there are no objections. It takes a few days for the approval to reach the Bhoomi kiosk, where it is scanned on the day of its arrival. An inward and outward register is maintained.

The updated RTC is printed at the Bhoomi kiosk and handed over to the village accountant for his record. The new owner receives a copy on demand. Bhoomi kiosks create scanned copies of the original mutation orders and notices to avoid unnecessary litigation due to claims that the notices were not served.

With the computerized system, administrators can quickly determine the number of approved and overdue mutation orders. Information collected from one urban taluk indicates that earlier 3,000 mutations were handled annually. After computerization, there is a 50 per cent jump in the number of mutation requests. This change would seem to indicate a level of approval of the new system by the population, and willingness to update changes in landownership that were previously left undocumented.

The Bhoomi software incorporates the bio-logon metrics system which authenticates all users of the software using their fingerprint. A log is maintained of all transactions in a session. This makes an officer accountable for his decisions and actions. The government also has plans to web-enable the database to make available to the farmer a copy of the land record locally through an Internet kiosk – although without signature such a copy will only have an informative value.

Problems Encountered at the Time of Computerization

Roll-out of the application to 177 locations has been a challenge due to the poor quality of manual records and the enormity of the data entry task. In the first phase, the project was implemented on a pilot basis in a controlled environment at four taluks. After gaining experience in data entry operations and implementation of the software, the scheme was extended to one pilot taluk in each of the 27 districts. In the third phase, the project is being rolled out simultaneously to all the remaining 177 taluks.

Records in the field were not up-to-date due to poor work culture and lack of training amongst the revenue staff. Also farmers often do not report transactions within the family, either because they are discouraged by the attitude of the revenue staff or due to internal family problems. The maintenance of land records is not uniform across districts.

As revenue officials were not interested in data entry, private data entry agencies tackled the 20,000 man-months of work in an off-line mode at the taluk level. A comprehensive software that accommodated all variations in manual records across districts was used. After the initial data entry, prints were validated against the original record books by the village accountants. Many problems were encountered in off-line data entry. The process was slow and error prone due to poor work quality by data entry agencies. Technical guidance from officers of the district informatics centre was not easily available as they were overloaded with other work. And data entry agencies were unwilling to recruit more manpower as it required investment in training on a specialized data entry software, which would not be useful to them for other projects. Moreover, interruptions in electrical power in taluk headquarters and delay in maintenance of computers at taluk level by vendors are a problem. Every district was provided with a consultant to act as a bridge between the data entry agency and the district administration. After the system is operational, the consultant trains the taluk staff and helps the district administration in day-to-day work at the Bhoomi kiosk.

The village accountants who would be in charge of the new kiosks were chosen very carefully. Young persons fresh out of college were recruited and trained at the headquarters. These officials had not experienced the power that a village accountant could exercise over rural farmers. The project leader (additional secretary of the department) personally participated in the training given to every batch of accountants, to ensure that they felt complete ownership and a sense of importance in being assigned to this new initiative. Accountants were encouraged to talk to the project leader either at his home or at his office. Nearly 500 officials, including all Deputy Tehsildars, were trained in the state headquarters, and more than 1,000 officials were trained by the Bhoomi consultants at the district level. The political executive was completely involved in the computerization project. All this helped demonstrate that there was a strong political will for computerization.

Economics of Cost-Benefit Analysis

The expenditure on data entry operations for about 2 million RTCs in 27 districts was Rs 80 million. The unit cost of providing hardware, construction of computer rooms and kiosks was of the order of Rs 0.64 million for each taluk. Thus, the total out-of-pocket expenditure on the project was Rs 185 million. This does not include the cost of software development done gratis by the National Informatics Centre, a department of the central government. The cost of processing an RTC has been roughly estimated at Rs 13, assuming a life of 5 years for the hardware and an activity level of 2 million RTCs issued from all the kiosks (10 per cent of all holdings). This cost includes an assumed operational expenditure of Rs 2 for stationery, cartridges and electricity. The current user fee of Rs 15 seems sufficient to cover these variable costs. However, if the scheme is extended to 700 sub-taluk offices, then there would be an additional expenditure of Rs 0.25 million per kiosk on hardware: 1 PC – Rs 45, 000, Printer – Rs 20, 000, UPS – Rs 5, 000, Generator – Rs 30, 000 and site preparation, raising the unit cost of processing to Rs 15 per record.

The total cost of the Bhoomi project till now stands at Rs 10 crore. The project demolishes the myth that people are unwilling to pay for a service. Five million farmers have already used the service, paying Rs 7.5 crore, thereby making it one of those rare self-sustaining government ventures. According to Mr Chawla, the full impact of the project will only be felt in the next 5-6 years. "It takes some time to get new ideas to sink in before it becomes part of everyday existence". On utilizing the data for a variety of purposes, Mr Chawla said: "Once we have the ownership and crop details, it doesn't take much effort to calculate the disposable income. I can easily calculate how much disposable income a person with 5 acre of sugarcane can generate. The same can be applied to any other crop". Bhoomi has won the Silver Award in the prestigious CAPAM international innovation Award for the year 2002, initiated by the Common Wealth Association of Public Administration and Management.

The State Government has already recovered Rs 11 crore of the total Rs 18 crore spent on Bhoomi land records project, Now the land records are in the public domain. Any record can be viewed through a touch screen at the kiosk. On an experimental basis, scanned maps of plots are being printed on the opposite side of the RTC printout in some of the taluks.

Farmers can apply for mutation and expedite the process by reviewing the status of their request online, presenting documentary evidence to supervisors in the event that their request is not processed within the stipulated time period.

Potential Future Benefits

There are plans to use the Bhoomi kiosk for disseminating other information, like lists of destitute and handicapped pensioners, families living below the poverty line, concessional foodgrain card holders, mandi rates and weather information. The system generates various types of reports on land ownership by size, type of soil, crops, owner's sex, etc., which would be useful for planning poverty alleviation programmes, and supplying agricultural inputs. Banks and other lending institutions could be provided electronic access to the database for processing requests for crop loans, and conduct some advance planning on the quantum of lending required. Similarly, high court, district and taluk courts could access the database for resolving legal disputes surrounding land. The system could also lead to better administration of Land Reforms Act, such as enforcing a ceiling on land holdings, etc.

From Table 6.1, it can be observed that number of farmers who availed services of Bhoomi from its inception till May 2003 is 98.18 lakh. The cumulative user charges collected from them is Rs 14.72 crore. It indicates that within a span of 3-4 years, 75 per cent of the total cost was collected in the form of user charges in the Bhoomi project. Out of this total collection, highest amount of user charges collected is from the districts of Belgaum, Bagalkot and Hassan in view of large number of farmers who availed the services. However, if we consider the availing of the service during May month it is evident that again farmers in Belgaum district constitutes 11.63 per cent to the total followed by Gulbarga, Mysore and other districts. The illiteracy in the backward region like Gulbarga did not come in the way of availing the services of e-governance projects in Karnataka.

Table 6.1

User Charges Collected from Bhoomi Kiosks Since its Inception and during May 2003

No.	District	Farmers who availed services from inception	Cumulative user charges collected	percentage to the grand total	Farmers who availed services during May '03	User charges collected during May '03	Percentage to the grand total
1.	Bangalore (Rural)	339258	5088870	3.46	19983	299745	3.06
2.	Bangalore (Urban)	341076	5116133	3.47	19705	295575	3.02
3.	Bagalkot	618536	9278040	6.30	27322	409830	4.19
4.	Belgaum	844463	12666950	8.60	75903	1138545	11.63
5.	Bellary	320189	4802840	3.26	23739	356085	3.64
6.	Bidar	233600	3504005	2.38	15282	229230	2.34
7.	Bijapur	501993	7529890	5.11	23969	359540	3.67
8.	Chamrajnagar	110894	1663410	1.13	8802	132030	1.35
9.	Chickmaglur	320927	4813900	3.27	20010	300145	3.07
10.	Chitradurga	291600	4374000	2.97	13331	199965	2.04
11.	Dakshin Kannada	446516	6697745	4.55	20119	301785	3.08
12.	Davanagere	397645	5964670	4.05	18606	279085	2.85
13	Dharwad	212079	3181185	2.16	19565	293475	3.00
14.	Gadag	197651	2964760	2.01	9394	140915	1.44
15.	Gulbarga	415206	6228092	4.23	40821	612320	6.25
16.	Hassan	589031	8835469	6.00	34215	513220	5.24
17.	Haveri	261163	3917445	2.66	20924	313855	3.21
18.	Kodagu	162985	2444775	1.66	101187	152805	1.56
19.	Kolar	333946	5009194	3.40	22485	337276	3.44
20.	Koppal	214360	3215402	2.18	10112	151675	1.55
21.	Mandya	443034	6645515	4.51	22357	335355	3.43
22.	Mysore	401003	6015045	4.08	57021	855315	8.74
23.	Raichur	259424	3891366	2.64	16286	244285	2.50
24.	Shimoga	408857	6132860	4.16	23718	355770	3.63
25.	Tumkur	559042	8385635	5.69	27192	407880	4.17
26.	Uttar Kannada	369522	5542835	3.76	34044	510665	5.22
27.	Udupi	224451	3366765	2.29	17620	264300	2.70
	Grand Total	9818453	147276796	100.00	652711	9790671	100.00

Source: Computed from the records of Revenue Department, Government of Karnataka as well as from website: www.revdept.kar.nic.in

Public-Private Partnership

Implementation of land record computerization has been difficult in India. Bhoomi succeeded because, extensive public-private partnership training coupled with a participatory style also helped to diminish resistance.

Project managers need to balance the potential benefits against the risk of implementation failure in deciding how much reform (re-engineering) to tackle at any one time. In Bhoomi, significant benefits are delivered in issuing RTCs, but much of the old mutation process remains unaltered. As there is no change in the role of the revenue inspector in passing the mutation order, corruption in the mutation process may not necessarily reduce. Bhoomi has reduced the discretion of public officials by introducing provisions for recording a mutation request online.

Farmers can now access the database and are empowered to follow up. Reports on overdue mutations can point to errant behaviour. Still, supervisors must examine the reports and take appropriate action. In remote areas, operators may turn away citizens by telling that the system offering online service is down. Strict field supervision is needed (through empowered citizens committees and NGOs) to curb such behaviour. Ultimately, the only recourse that a citizen has against such practices is to lodge a complaint. The process for lodging a complaint should be facilitated through the web. The backend has to be geared up to handle complaints received electronically.

As an implementation strategy, manually written RTCs were declared illegal from the day on which the computerized system became operational in a taluka. This forced the department and the farmers to completely rely on the new system. The strategy worked because the application design was robust and did not falter.

However, an independent audit is required to measure the improvements and collect feedback from all stakeholders – something that is not done for most projects. In any case, the system should be allowed to stabilize and prove its sustainability over a two-year period before attempting its replication. Therefore, a field level study was undertaken by the researcher in the state of Karnataka during December 2003.

A Field Level Study: Welfare Gain and Loss to Farmers from 'Bhoomi' Project

In order to critically evaluate the benefits reaped by the farmers and the problems faced by them in accessing the benefits, a sample of 100 farmers, 40 from Belgaum division (due to large number of farmers who availed this service) and 20 each from Gulbarga, Bangalore Rural, and Mysore divisions were interviewed with structured questionnaire during the month of December 2003. The results are quite interesting and appealing. Of course, they do face some problems and therefore suggestions are offered to improve the system.

Welfare Gain

(1) The general profile of the beneficiaries of e-governance Bhoomi project in Karnataka depicted in Table 6.2 reveals that the farmers from all the divisions of Karnataka belonged to different categories across different size group of land. Table 6.2 also indicates that farmers belonging to OBC groups are more in number (46) followed by SC/ST (28) and general category (26).

Table 6.2

General Profile of the Beneficiaries of 'Bhoomi' E-Governance Project in Karnataka during 2003-04

Division	*No. of sample farmers*	*Size of their lands*			*Category*		
		1-5 acres	*5-10 acres*	*10 and above*	*Gen*	*ST/ST*	*OBC*
Bangalore	20	10	4	6	2	6	12
Mysore	20	18	2	–	–	2	18
Belgaum	40	20	10	10	14	16	10
Gulbarga	20	4	8	8	10	4	6
Total	100	52	24	24	26	28	46

Source: Computed from the field data.

(2) As far as classification of purpose of obtaining RTC by farmers is concerned (Table 6.3) 52 out of 100 farmers have obtained RTC for the purpose of crop loan followed by 22 for income/caste certificate, 12 for court bail application and 12 for scholarship of their children. Since the crop loan is availed by the farmer every year, the need for RTC is imminent and thus getting RTC in a single day at affordable cost is a real welfare gain to the farmers. The introduction of computer based RTC to the farmers in Karnataka has delivered some welfare gain. But, the gain varied between the large and small farmers. It is heartening to note that *welfare gain is more to small farmers than large farmers*, because small farmers do require RTC twice or thrice in a year for getting crop loan from banks in two or three instalments. They were supposed to meet village accountants more than once. While large farmers required RTC once in a year for their medium and long-term loan and used to meet village accountants only once (and pay bribe).

Table 6.3

Classification of Purposes of Obtaining RTC by the Sample Farmers

Division	*Crop loan purpose (No. of farmers)*	*Income/ caste certificate*	*For mutation*	*Scholarship for children*	*Court bail application*
Bangalore	14	4	2	–	-
Mysore	6	8	–	4	2
Belgaum	22	6	–	2	10
Gulbarga	10	4	–	6	–
Total	52	22	2	12	12

Source: Computed from the field data.

Now farmers can directly go to kiosk and get the computerized RTC printout by just paying Rs 15 after the entry of their land survey number and name of the village. Earlier, it was very difficult to meet the village accountants as they used to visit 3-4 villages. Therefore, frequent travel by farmers is avoided.

In case a farmer wants to get medium and long-term loans from a particular bank, he has to produce RTC of previous 10-12 years. Earlier, the farmer used to pay a bribe amount of anywhere between Rs 1,000 to 5,000 as the official had to open the old records from the record room. The urgency of the record used to heighten the rate of corruption. Now getting RTC of previous 3 years is not a problem. By paying Rs 15 for one year (total Rs 45 for 3 years) he can get 3 years RTCs. Thus, large-gain welfare is noticed in case of farmers availing medium and long-term loan.

(3) Table 6.4 depicts that the amount of money (including transport cost) spent by farmers during 1999-00 and 2000-01 was in the order of Rs 3,722 and Rs 4,880 respectively. This is a little higher amount than the amount of Rs 1,600 and Rs 1,680 during the period of 2002-03 and 2003-04. The per head cost of obtaining RTC works out to be Rs 372 to Rs 488 before computerization while Rs 160 to Rs 168 after computerization. It clearly indicates that there is a real monetary gain to the farmers.

Table 6.4

Comparison of Amount Spent by Farmers to Get Hand Written/Computerized RTC in the Study Area

(in Rs)

Division	*Amount spent to get hand written RTC*		*Amount spent to get computerized RTC*	
	1999-00	*2000-01*	*2002-03*	*2003-04*
Bangalore	827	1308	300	300
Mysore	730	812	300	300
Belgaum	1925	2400	600	600
Gulbarga	240	360	400	480
Total	3722	4880	1600	1680

Source: Computed from the field data.

(4) Regarding the level of harassment, Table 6.5 reveals that as many as 72 out of 100 farmers felt that there is low harassment compared to earlier period. Across the divisions, all the 20 respondents in Gulbarga division expressed happiness and said that high level of harassment is nil.

Table 6.5

Number of Farmers Responded Towards the Level of Harassment by Village Accountant and Revenue Inspector in Getting RTC Before and After Computerization

Division	*Level of Harassment*					
	Before			*After*		
	High	*Low*	*Medium*	*High*	*Low*	*Medium*
Bangalore	18	–	2	–	16	4
Mysore	8	10	2	2	12	6
Belgaum	24	8	8	4	24	12
Gulbarga	6	6	8	–	20	–
Total	56	24	20	6	72	22

Source: Computed from the field data.

Further, Table 6.6 indicates that the average time required to obtain RTC was minimum of 5-10 days during the earlier period compared to one day after computerization. This seems to be a big welfare gain to farmers.

(5) As far as mutation is concerned, there is absolutely no welfare gain to any farmers. Because mutation still is in the hands of revenue officials. When the mutation copy is produced only then there is an entry in the computer. As a result, there is not much difference in spending money for mutation purpose either before or after computerization. The cost hovers on an average of Rs 2,472 to 2,600 per person in a year (see Table 6.7) though the number of days to obtain certificate might have been reduced.

Table 6.6

Farmer's Responses about Manipulation of Land Records and Time Required to Obtain RTC in the Study Area

Division	*Manipulation in land records*				*Average time required to obtain RTC*	
	Then		*Now*		*HW*	*At compu-kiosk*
	Yes	*No*	*Yes*	*No*	*2001*	*2002*
Bangalore	20	–	2	18	5 days	1 day
Mysore	14	6	6	14	10 days	1 day
Belgaum	34	6	16	24	10 days	1 day
Gulbarga	20	–	2	18	15 days	1 day
Total	88	12	26	74		

Source: Computed from field data.

Note: HW – Hand Written.

Table 6.7

Farmer's Response About the Number of Days and Amount Spent in Land Record Transfer (Mutation) from Owner/Parent to Purchaser/Children Respectively per Person in the Study Area During December 2003

Division	*Mutation Purpose (per person)*			
	Before Computerization		*After Computerization*	
	Days	*Amt (Rs)*	*Days*	*Amt (Rs)*
Bangalore	60	1150	35	1150
Mysore	60	2250	45	2250
Belgaum	80	2270	50	3000
Gulbarga	90	3800	40.	4000
Total/Average	72	2472	42	2600

Source: Computed from field data.

(6) Though manipulation of land records is not possible now, there are some instances of manipulation of RTC, which was questioned in the courts by the farmers and cases are now pending in courts. This has happened due to highly corrupt revenue officials. The avoidance of manipulation itself is a big welfare gain to farmers in Karnataka.

(7) Welfare gain to institutions is another interesting fact. Earlier, village accountants used to issue RTC by changing the numbers slightly and gaining the money by doing this favour (for example, if one survey No. is 420, that RTC is pledged in one bank. Next if another is needed, RTC is issued as survey No. 420/A and given to the farmer to get another loan from another bank). As a result, the farmers were over indebted. This burden of debt lead them to suicides. In Karnataka, during 2001-02 drought, nearly 250 farmers committed suicide. Most of them were highly indebted and belong to irrigated area. Now computerized RTC has completely eradicated this bogus issue of RTCs and consequent involvement of farmers in the misuse of bank loan.

Welfare Loss

(1) Though there is a 'good feel factor' to the majority of the farmers in getting the RTC without any harassment, but in monetary terms there is some loss to them. Since most of the kiosks are at the place of a taluk (sub-district level), every farmer has to travel from his village to the taluk office. He has to incur not only travel cost but also other incidental expenses towards tea, meals, etc., and also has to loose one days wage/work during his visit. Therefore, almost all (100) respondents felt that the kiosk should be at the Hobli or panchayat level.

(2) Since the computer operators are working as part-time workers on consolidated salary of Rs 2,000-3,000, sometimes they play truant on the excuse of technical deficiency or lack of electricity or something else. Some of

the respondents expressed that the extra money is demanded for urgent issue of RTC.

(3) Since the farmers are illiterate they do not remember the survey number of their own piece of land. Again, they have to approach village accountant and get the number. Only after providing the survey number and paying a fee of Rs 15, farmer get a computerized RTC. Thus, illiteracy among farmers many times takes away the possible gain from the kiosk. This illiteracy and ignorance give scope for the middle man, therefore, still there are mediators exploiting the farmers in the system. Though the extent of corruption in getting the RTC is minimized, the same is not true in case of mutation (transfer of rights from one owner to another or from parents to their children). Here things will not move without the bribe to be paid. There is no difference in the situation between the period of hand written mutation and computerized mutation. In fact, there is no automatic mutation through the computer. Hence, corruption still exists or has increased in magnitude in certain cases. At present, four persons are involved in issue of mutation, viz., village accountant at village level, revenue inspector at Hobli level, case worker in taluk office and tehsildar at the final stage. The application has to pass through all these and then after 30 days of notice, entry will be made in computer. This cumbersome procedure breeds corruption. Hence, as soon as the sale deed is obtained along with RTC and prescribed fee receipt, entry can be effected through scanning in the computer and mutation certificate can be issued.

(4) The installed 'touch-screen facility' exists in one or two revenue divisions and its use is not frequently done by farmers. It does not serve the purpose, except that they can just view the RTC on the computer. Hence, authorities should try to replace it by scanning machine. Scanning machine may be helpful in processing of application at the time of issue of mutation certificate.

Conclusion

The overall feeling of the respondent farmers in Karnataka is satisfactory with a rider. Unanimously they said that the computerized RTC facility is good and helpful but it should be in their own panchayat office/Hobli place so that they can avoid the cost of transport and loss of day's work. Further, in order to avoid corruption at mutation level, there is a need to make a provision for entry in the computer of sale deed or *khota* transfer application through scanning and total transparency has to be maintained.

There are other possibilities that could make RTCs available at sub-taluk level. For example, an unsigned copy can be made available from an Internet kiosk with some official seal. If such copies can be accepted by banks and verified by accessing the departmental database, the need for signed copies will be reduced. A solution may emerge through wider consultations with the ultimate consumers of these documents. About 5.6 million farmers have visited Bhoomi kiosks and the system is slowly establishing social equity among the landed class in the State. Self-sustainability is the hallmark of the Bhoomi project, and countries like Sri Lanka and Cambodia are now studying the structure for application in their own contexts.

Comments

The Bhoomi project has been critically evaluated by several economists who questioned the whole truth about it and said it is a hype. The main difference between Karnataka and Andhra Pradesh is that the latter is better coordinated and the concerned officers do their homework well. The Andhra Pradesh government has created the post of Chief Information Officers (CIOs), at a fairly senior level, who have undergone thorough training in managing information technology projects. They are to initiate and take up ownership of ICT projects. The classic example of Andhra Pradesh doing its homework is the existence of an information technology infrastructure framework. An intensive exercise was carried out through which, with help of consultants, information technology architecture has been designed; all ICT initiatives of the state are expected to conform to this framework. The idea of CIOs is yet to take off in Karnataka and there does not seem to be much enthusiasm about it.

In the world of software development, one speaks of measuring oneself on the Capability Maturity Model (CMM). It has five levels – the lower most, called 'initial' is at level 1 and the highest, called 'optimizing' is at level 5. Karnataka is at level 1 and Andhra Pradesh is at level 2 (called the 'repeatable' level of maturity). Translation of this means that most of Karnataka's development in ICT is 'ad hoc' and that Andhra Pradesh, while not fully mature, is one level higher. Repeatable, implies some procedural discipline (Jagdish, 2003).

If the Bhoomi project in Karnataka is to serve the total needs of the farmer in the state, it has to go beyond just land records and treat the farmer as a valuable customer. Bhoomi, unfortunately, stands as an island – there are too many medium sized and small projects that are floating around, almost rudderless one must say. The right hand, often, does not know what the left hand is doing. Interestingly, under the aegis of another project, one of the government departments had already engaged a vendor to create digital maps of districts. They could have as well been used by this project but they had no idea of its existence. Information sharing across departments is minimal (Kulkarni, 2003).

In the near future, spatial data will have to be linked to Bhoomi to allow scanning of old records and a 're-survey' of land, apart from linking the Bhoomi database to 2,500 bank branches to simplify farm credit procedures. Similarly, courts would be connected to facilitate faster disposal of land disputes. The government can also distribute Simputer-like hand-held devices to village accountants to collect crop data and thus include the whole set of Bhoomi data in the planning process. The government should think of more flexible and proactive methods of partnering with vendors if they have to get their projects implemented on time.

E-Governance Project in Andhra Pradesh

Andhra Pradesh is another state, which made a dent in the field of e-governance. The ICT Policy, 2002-05 provides several incentives. Some of the e-government projects now implemented in different areas in the state are APSWAN (Andhra Pradesh State Wide Area Network), CARD (Computer Aided Registration Department), e-Seva, FAST (Fully Automated Services of Transport), APDMS (Andhra Pradesh Development Monitoring System), SKIMS (Secretariat Knowledge and Information System) and MPHS (Multipurpose Household Survey Project). The efficacy and transparency achieved through these projects needs to be scrutinized more thoroughly based on the experience gained so far. Under APSWAN, 25 towns including 23 district headquarters are connected with the state secretariat. Eventually, all the towns and 1,107 mandal headquarters in the state will be covered in this project. The project envisages simultaneous communication of vast amounts of data, voice and video transmission. The Chief Minister, ministers and other higher officials in Hyderabad can hold statewide conferences, and district officials can hold interactive sessions with other officials at short notices and access vast quantities of information simultaneously, which will save time and money by avoiding travel and related expenses. Already, video conferencing from Hyderabad with district officials and teleconferencing from district headquarters with mandal offices has become quite a routine practice in the state. While this practice is allowing instant interaction and saving time, there are apprehensions of the decision-making power getting concentrated at higher levels.

E-Seva Project in Andhra Pradesh

Among all the 'e-government' initiatives, the e-Seva seems to be getting popular with the urban middle classes in twin cities of

Hyderabad and Secunderabad. This is a one-stop-shop for citizen services. It is providing a wide spectrum of citizen friendly services like utility bills/tax payments, issue of certificates, issue of licences/permits, reservations and more on a one-stop basis. The e-Seva is a government organization built on public-private partnership model. Citizens are provided with a clean, transparent, efficient and effective administrative system through the state-of-the-art electronic technology. It provides a direct interface between the citizens and the government which saves considerable time, energy and money to everyone and gives the citizens the advantage of hassle-free dealings with the administration.

Highlights of the E-Seva Project

The main objective of this scheme is to improve the quality of Government to Citizen (G2C) service delivery in the state and to provide an effective and transparent government to citizens of the state using the information technology as the tool.

- All services can be availed at any centre.
- All services can be availed at any counter within the centre, i.e., a consumer need not visit one counter for one service and another for another service.
- There are no jurisdictional limits.
- Services can be availed on holidays as well.
- Bill payments can be made over the Internet.
- Development of Integrated Citizen Service Centre (ICSC) to offer services of multiple government departments under one roof.
- Payment of utility bills like water, electricity, telephone, property tax, etc.
- Issue of birth, death and property certificates.
- Booking bus tickets and train tickets.
- Issue of trade licence.
- Filing of passport application.
- Sale of legal documents for land registration.

- Sale of state tourism department's travel and entertainment packages.
- Integrated caste, nativity and birth certificate based on SSID number.
- Filing of income tax returns.
- Sale of judicial stamps.
- Filing of A2 and C6 monthly returns by dealers.
- Market value assistance to know the prevailing market price of lands.

The e-Seva data centre communicates with the servers of the departments concerned. Therefore, payment particulars get updated on the departmental servers in real time. About 20,000 citizens transact at the e-Seva centres everyday. Citizens can use the facilities through the net by online payments, e-Seva receipt is treated as a conclusive proof of payment

Speaking on the occasion, Phani Kumar, Project Director, e-Seva said: "The State of Andhra Pradesh is synonymous with information technology and the e-Seva project is reflective of our commitment to citizen care. Being pioneers, it was important to ensure that the project delivered on its promise to our citizens for which a robust and reliable backend was imperative. And Cisco with its clear focus on customer care and end-to-end solutions was an obvious partner of choice."

Comments

What is lacking is a system of information technology applications that will directly benefit the agriculture sector and reduce rural poverty. The state is also lacking in the kind of projects that are being initiated in Madhya Pradesh and Uttar Pradesh for rural development. The state's approach on 'information technology and poverty reduction' has no focused agenda. The stress seems to be on several sectors which, if developed, are going to have an indirect impact on poverty reduction. For example, the statement, "use of information technology for enhancing agricultural production and productivity could have an immediate impact on the poverty reduction" (Sudan 2001), may mean nothing in the absence of a concrete and workable policy in this direction. It is pointed that "in the absence of a broad attack on poverty and illiteracy", the Andhra Pradesh government's strategy is forced to rely on the 'trickle-down' effects of ICT.

The Comptroller and Auditor General of India (CAG), in its report, charged the Andhra Pradesh government with starting the e-Seva project without any formal budget provision and without conducting a feasibility study: "The financial rules were largely neglected by the director in implementing the programme".

The state government presented the CAG audit report for the year ended March 31, 2002 to the Andhra Pradesh Legislative Assembly. CAG said that the project has suffered from lack of transparency, inefficient and ineffective implementation due to unpreparedness of the participating departments and inadequate coordination. "The report also expressed fears over the integrity, reliability and safety of the data across the project. The e-governance project was rushed through even when the participating departments were not ready."

However, CAG looks from the angle of rules of finance and not from the services received by the public. The state government is offering about 42 services, both government and private, over the e-Seva platform covering about 20-odd counters in Hyderabad and had proposed to open over 120 urban and semi-urban centres across the state. Besides, the services will be offered through private operators who can convert their STD booths into e-Seva centres in the rural areas. In this context, the comments of Atal Behari Vajpayee, while inaugurating the 22nd Conference of CAG of India in New Delhi on 29 August 2003, is worth noting. To quote:

> The executive becomes a prisoner of procedures, rather than achiever of purpose. An atmosphere in which the auditor is on the offensive and the executive is on the defensive is detrimental to good performance...in the absence of timely decisions and

programmes become victims of unacceptable time and cost overrun.

He suggested that the audit of the CAG should not be seen as a mere fault finding exercise but should be looked at a useful mechanism for correction and reconstruction. "A change in the mindset of auditors is required as the overall objective is to enhance substantially the delivery capability for accelerating the overall development". Therefore, the comments of the CAG cannot be taken seriously and one cannot undermine the importance of e-governance projects rendering the service to the citizens.

E-Governance Project in Madhya Pradesh

While Andhra Pradesh and Karnataka are seemingly vying with each other for the number one position, much has been achieved very silently by another state. Madhya Pradesh took a great march over both of them by sneaking from behind and winning the International Stockholm award in the year 2000 as the best ICT project in development for its 'Gyandoot' in India. It is a low cost e-governance initiative that has helped rural folk in the district of Dhar in Madhya Pradesh (Jagdish, 2003).

Gyandoot Project

Gyandoot (which literally means, 'ambassador of knowledge') is a unique form of G2C (Government to Citizen) e-commerce activity being performed in Madhya Pradesh, wherein the local elected governing council is enabling rural tribal citizens affordable access to various government and market related needs through economically viable state-of-the-art information technology. It was started in November 1999.

Brief Project Summary

Gyandoot is in the tribal district of Dhar in Central India. It is a community-based, highly cost-effective and financially self-reliant approach to bring the benefits of information technology to the doorsteps of tribal villagers. It is about economic growth, government-citizen partnership and devolution of public offices to every network computer terminal. The people take full charge of running, developing and supporting the network on a sustainable basis. The people also take charge of their own knowledge and transfer of technology needs, narrowing the gap between the knows and know-nots. In its essence, the Gyandoot project is an intranet network of 26 soochanalayas (information centres) set up at the cost of just Rs 25 lakh, that benefit nearly half a million people at 311 Gram Panchayats in over 600 villages.

The villagers are able to access any information like mandi prices of crops, copies of land records, grievance redressal, sending in e-mails in their language, apply for assistance under government schemes, get their health records accessed through the main hospital at Indore, etc. The government has only played the role of the facilitator in this project. In fact, even the sum of Rs 25 lakh that has been spent on the project was raised through the district's own resources. The centres are managed by 'soochaks', who are local folks, and are not government employees. The maintenance of the network has also been handed over to a private entrepreneur.

Connectivity was offered either in terms of dial-up telephone lines, or Cordect's WiLL (wireless-in local loop), a technology from the Indian Institute of Technology, Chennai, which is working to boost rural Internet accessibility across India. The stereotypical image of the illiterate villager shuffling around the corridors of 'babudom' in search of documents or records could well be over. The Indian village is getting wired for empowerment. It is this change that makes Madhya Pradesh the right place for information technology for millions. Obviously, the Gyandoot experience is being extended to other districts, and the opportunities are opening up for the investors in the information technology-related activities.

Highlights of the Gyandoot Project

- Gyandoot stresses the importance of putting out information available about government schemes' issues in various forms.
- It also offers certificates of income, caste and domicile and details about land-records.
- Complaints to officials about social atrocities, or petition the government on various issues that require redressal, can be filed using these kiosks.
- Copies of document like the 'citizens charters' can be obtained (which guide on what the official duties and responsibilities of government departments)
- An important feature of Gyandoot is that it allows citizens to ask questions. This is called 'Sawaali Raam se puchiyee' (Ask What You Wish).
- Gives the list of below poverty line.
- Rural matrimonial and employment news is also provided.

These computers have been established in Gram Panchayats. They have been called soochanalayas, which are located either at block headquarters or at prominent *haat bazaar* or at prominent villages on major roads which are important from the point of catching the bus, etc. Thus, each soochanalaya caters to approximately15 Gram Panchayats and about 25 to 30 villages. The benefits cover wide-ranging information needs of all villagers, not merely those belonging to cooperatives. From the soochanalaya, user-charge based services are given to the masses and at the same time the information technology related developmental needs of government departments and Panchayats are met free of cost.

Soochanalyas

Soochanalayas are 26 client sites/nodes working as rural cyber cafe-cum-cyber offices. Each soochanalaya provides services to 20,000 to 30,000 population. The Intranet will cover 5 out of 13 blocks in the district and 3 out of 7 tehsils in the district in the initial phase. The soochanalayas are located on the roadside and are central villages where people normally travel to.

Soochanalayas have telephone line connectivity to begin with. The hardware is procured and given to the Gram Panchayat under agreement with the Zila Panchayat. The Gram Panchayat in turn gives it for operation to the soochak under agreement. The Gram Panchayat provides, readies and maintains the building where the soochanalaya is housed. It also provides the telephone and electric connection as well as the furniture.

Soochana Kosh

Server/hub, i.e., Remote Access Server (RAS) housed in the computer room in Zila Panchayat is called Soochana Kosh.

Soochak

An important aspect of the scheme is that the person selected to operate the soochanalaya is a local youth from the same village who was trained to run the soochanalaya. These operators, called soochaks run the soochanalaya on commercial lines and generate income and livelihood for themselves. Soochak is not an employee but an entrepreneur. Soochak only needs maintenance and numeric data entry skills. He needs very limited typing skills since most of the intranet software is menu-driven. He is similar to an STD booth operator. Most of the youth selected for soochanalayas had never seen a computer. They were all trained at the Zila Panchayat. They were given 7 days training in three stages at their own expenses by computer operators of DRDA. The soochaks were selected interactively by Gram Panchayat along with representatives from the Zila Panchayat. Three member panels were selected who received training at their own cost at the Zila Panchayat. At the end of the training, the best trainees were selected as soochaks. He/she will run the soochanalaya at his own cost. He will be working according to an initial one year agreement with the Gram Panchayat. He will bear the cost of stationery, maintenance and electric and telephone bills. He will pay 10 per cent of income as commission to the Zila Panchayat for maintaining the net. Each soochak is expected to earn a net income of at least Rs 24,000 per annum; at conservative estimate.

In all the soochanalaya villages, three meetings each were organized with the villagers where in-depth participatory appraisal was done. The design of the services provided was a result of this interactive exercise and was based upon the advice and the felt needs of the villagers. In these meetings, it was learned that due to lack of information regarding the proper 'mandi' rates not only in the local mandis but in the benchmark mandis (where the local mandi trader sells his own purchases), the farmers are unable to get the best prices for their agricultural produce. Villagers also informed that copies of land records are difficult to obtain since the 'patwari' is often on tour and one patwari is responsible for several villages. The villager needing a copy of the land records has to go out in search of the patwari who may or may not be available on that particular day at his headquarters. For small complaints or for giving applications, people had to go to block, tehsil or district headquarters which resulted in waste of time, money and potential livelihood earnings.

From the soochanalayas, rates of grains and vegetables of nearly a dozen mandis, copies of revenue maps or *khasras* or B1 may be obtained. On the preparation of the desired certificate/*rin pustika,* the information will be sent through e-mail to the concerned soochanalaya. These will be prepared in a maximum period of 10 day. Complaints regarding government schemes/programmes/institutions/employees may also be sent through the net and in a maximum period of seven days, reply regarding their disposal will be sent back to the concerned soochanalaya.

Information of Mandi Prices

The variety-wise rates of 15 prominent cereal crops of the district like wheat, gram, soyabean, etc., and today's rates of local Dhar, Badnawar and Indore mandis as well as the volumes of incoming agricultural produce are provided to the villagers from soochanalayas at a charge of Rs 5. These rates are quoted for nearby Dahod as well as distant Mumbai and Delhi mandis. The previous two days' rates are also given.

Horticulture crops like tomato, potato, peas, green chillies and guava are also produced in substantial quantity in the district. The rates of these commodities are provided in case of Ratlam, Indore, Chennai, Ahmedabad, Mumbai, Delhi and Hyderabad mandis. These rates are also given at a charge of Rs 5.

Copies of Khasra, B1/Khatauni and Map

Documents relating to farmer's land including map, *khasra* and B1 are given on the spot at a charge of Rs 15 per extract. All the banks in the district have agreed to accept extracts issued from soochanalayas for the purposes of banking transactions. Farmers need these extracts every *kharif* and *rabi* season to obtain crop loans from banks for purchasing seeds and fertilizers.

On-Line Registration Applications

So far, the villagers had to go to the tehsil court to file applications for obtaining income/caste/domicile certificates or for getting demarcation done or for obtaining landholder's loan passbook (*rin pustika*). For this, they would again make repeated visits to the court to enquire about the progress of the application as well as to finally collect the prepared document. Now, through soochanalayas they may send the application at a cost of only Rs 10 and thereafter, in a maximum period of 10 days, an intimation of the readiness of the certificate would be sent back to them through e-mail at the concerned soochanalaya. Thereafter, they may go to the concerned court to collect the certificate.

Public Grievance Redressal

Wherever there is some problem in the delivery of services, the villagers travel at the cost of time, money and livelihood to

Block, tehsil or district headquarters without any certainty that they would even be able to meet the officer concerned. Now through the soochanalaya, the villager may send his/her complaint with assurance of reply within a maximum period of seven days, preferably lesser, at a charge of Rs 10. The reply of the disposal of his complaint may be received back at the soochanalaya through e-mail.

Complaints include handpump disorder, teacher's absence, mid-day meal, scholarship sanction/disbursement, poor seed/fertilizer, employee establishment (matters like leave or provident fund sanction) queries, etc.

Hindi E-mail

The district and block levels may communicate in Hindi through e-mail amongst themselves.

Management Information System (MIS)

Through soochanalayas, a Management Information System (MIS) relating to health, education and Gram Panchayats is also being introduced in Dhar block. Through this MIS, the village level worker may directly send necessary information from nearby soochanalayas to the block and district level. The compilation and analysis of these data will enable better management of the activities of health and education departments as well as of Gram Panchayats. The three MIS will be entered directly by the concerned departmental functionary at the soochanalaya.

Brief Profile of the Recent Additions to the Gyandoot Intranet

Gram Daak

An e-mailing software which is all set to become the hotmail for villagers. Working in their local language, it has all the features and facilities of a state-of-the-art web based e-mail. In addition to this, gram daak also has a client version which works locally at the Gyandoot soochanalayas end and has message queuing facility. On getting connected, it transfers all the mails in the outbox of the Gyandoot server and receives the incoming mails stored therein. This reduces the burden on the perennially disturbed telephone connectivity.

Expansion in Availability of Rates for More Mandis and More Crops

State Mandi Board has begun supplying rates of wheat on the Gyandoot intranet for another 23 mandis, over and above the initial 13 mandis whose rates were provided earlier for varieties and crops. The Board will be adding information of rates of other varieties/crops also soon for the new 23 mandis. Rates of nine more varieties/crops have been added over and above the initial 15. Thus, rates of 24 crops/varieties from 13 mandis and rates of wheat from 36 mandis are now available.

Government Sponsored Loan Project Preparation and Submission

Villagers who seek government sponsored loans may get a project report prepared for occupations in the approved shelf of loan projects at the nearby soochanalaya and submit them there itself with necessary supporting documents for forwarding to banks/lending agency in case of the Swarnjayanti Gram Swarojgar Yojana (SGSY – the recast IRDP). The citizen need not hunt professionals for project preparation or case files from extension workers to desks, offices and sponsoring committees. The correct project may be prepared, approved and forwarded to the banks/lending agencies with reply assured within two weeks by visiting a soochanalaya for a modest fixed fee of Rs 25.

District Weather Report for Farmers

The daily weather forecast of Dhar district by the Meteorology Department, GoI, Bhopal office will me made available to farmers through Gyandoot soochanalayas before the end of July. The State Agriculture Department will also be providing agro-meteorological advice to farmers based on the weather report.

Avedan

Forms of everything ranging from taxes to government schemes and offices will be available within a week through the Gyandoot Intranet. The villagers will have access to all application forms required and necessary for panchayat to central government ranging from application for mutation of land to form for arms license.

Benefits Accrued to the People

Benefits accrued to the villagers have been culled out from the official records as well as news published in the dailies. Some of them are as follows:

(1) Farmers in village used to get Rs 300 per quintal from local traders for their potato crop. On taking the rate slip from the soochanalaya, the farmers could get Rs 400 per quintal at the current rate in Indore mandi. Due to this benefit, they are now taking their produce to Indore mandi.

(2) The release of State Finance Commission grants to Gram Panchayats is now intimated to them on the same day through e-mail. Ordinarily, the money transferred by the Zila Panchayat into the accounts of the Gram Panchayats was intimated either through post or in the monthly meeting of Gram Panchayat secretaries at the Block level, weeks after the actual transfer of funds. In the meantime, the Gram Panchayat did not even know that the money had reached its account. Besides resulting in delay of works, non-utilization of funds in time, it also resulted in the Sarpanch and the Gram Panchayat secretary unnecessarily doing rounds of offices of Zila Panchayat or the Block in the earlier system.

(3) In the interior remote hamlets the local guruji/teacher of Education Guarantee Scheme centres usually do not receive their honorarium in time. Upon receipt of this

complaint through the soochanalaya, the problem was promptly solved.

(4) A resident of Deharisarai village gave an application for scheduled caste certificate. The enclosures submitted by him along with the certificate at the soochanalaya were sufficient in themselves. As a result, immediately upon receipt of his e-mail his caste certificate could be prepared and intimation of preparation of caste certificate could be sent back promptly through e-mail.

(5) Similarly, different kinds of experiences and demands have come up at different soochanalayas. Private school operators approached the soochak for training school children on computers and desktop composing of question papers and report cards. The soochak being trained earlier in computers, started training of six rural youth. At several other places also youth and schools have approached soochanalayas for availing computer training. Training of government teachers using computers has begun. Students of class 11th are being given a brief visit to the soochanalaya so that in the summer vacation after the examinations they may take up computer training on their own.

(6) As many as 3,054 students have used the Gyandoot kiosks to access their school-leaving results. This meant that kiosk owners could earn Rs 30,000 – a tidy sum by local standards in just two days time. All this, by fulfilling a vital societal need for information. Also available are Agri-market rates and an online matrimonial service. These services come at a price-tag of between Rs 5 to 25. To help supplement their income, Gyandoot kiosk owners are encouraged to undertake job-work and typing tasks for the villagers.

Comments

This venture is not problem-free. It has to face some problems and future growth may be hindered if it is not set right early. These are:

Problem of Power Cut in Rural Area

Electricity is the most important problem. This area has regular power-cuts of up to 6 hours a day. And that is a scheduled power-cut. Besides, connectivity is also a problem. Sometimes, it is the entire telephone exchanges that go down not just a few lines. Lack of women's involvement is another issue. No doubt, keeping in view the widespread power-cuts in rural areas, the soochanalayas have been equipped with uninterrupted power supply (UPS) systems. The UPS system is just not enough to run the computer as well as the printer for more than five hours at a stretch from a battery. These UPS is to be charged on single phase electricity for 8 hours for running the computer.

Problem of Interest Rate Burden of Borrowed Loan

The funds for the Gyandoot network have come from existing untied funds available with the Panchayats. The sources of the funding are as follows:

- The revenues of Gram Panchayats deposited in Zila Panchayat Raj Nidhi.
- Annual State Finance Commission share of revenues of Gram Panchayats.
- NSAP administrative allotment of Zila and Janpada Panchayats.
- Advertisements on pre-printed stationery and website (Rs 78,000).

Since the entire expenditure has come from Panchayats, the system has been set up at no cost to the government exchequer. The cost of each additional centre is Rs 75,000. Private investors or people availing of bank loans may start such soochanalayas as the services given to the public from the soochanalayas are based upon user charge. However, if the scheme is independent of the government from an economic point of view, it is doubtful about financial self-sustainability due to poor basic infrastructure to the new centres. The problem of connectivity and power may create another problem of interest rate burden from the banks. The successful information technology system may be established in the rural areas more on the public-private partnership rather on private alone.

E-Governance Project in Maharashtra

E-governance initiatives in Maharashtra are mostly infrastructure and back office projects undertaken by forming alliances with public firms like C-DAC and CMC and private companies to develop e-governance solutions. However, in Warana, a village in Maharashtra, National Informatics Centre and the state government launched a project called Warana Wired Village (WWV) project. The primary objective of the project is to demonstrate the effective contribution of an information technology infrastructure in the accelerated socio-economic development of a cluster of 70 contiguous villages around Warana in the Kolhapur and Sangli districts. The project is being jointly carried out by NIC (on behalf of the central government), the government of Maharashtra and the Warana Vibhag Shikshan Mandal. The estimated cost of the project is around Rs 2.5 crore.

High-speed VSAT was used to allow Internet access to existing cooperative societies. The project aims to provide agricultural, medical, and education information to villagers by establishing networked 'facilitation booths' in the villages. All the villages in the area have computer kiosks that are linked to a central network, and training centres have been opened in six villages to impart computer education to rural youth and provide access to the Internet.

Warana's project is providing farmers with access to essential information. The network keeps detailed records of all transactions with local sugar and milk cooperatives; it lists prices of farm produce in the region's agricultural markets (to help farmers decide what to plant or where to sell their produce); and it offers a daily weather forecast.

The Warana cooperative complex is one of the finest examples of successful integrated rural development resulting from cooperative movement through peoples' participation. It comprises of 25 cooperative societies in the field of sugar, milk, poultry, house construction, etc., with a turnover of over Rs 600 crore. Needless to say, it offered a perfect set-up for initiating the Wired Village concept.

Highlights of the Project

- The project provides agricultural, medical and educational information to villagers by establishing networked 'facilitation booths' in all the 70 villages.
- Brings the world knowledge at the door-steps of Warana villagers through Internet via NICNET.
- Provides tele-education at both primary and higher level educational institutes.
- Develops user-friendly map based information systems for better administration.
- It has increased the efficiency/productivity of the existing cooperative societies and provided greater transparency in their working.

In all, the project aims at the higher goals of achieving computer literacy, generating employment, improving agricultural output and ensuring greater transparency in the administration of villages.

Application of the WWV Project

Agriculture Produce Market Information System for Warana

The scope of this application is to display the most recent market arrivals and rates of various regulated commodities for all the major Agriculture Produce Marketing Committees (APMC) in Maharashtra. The data covers the quantity of arrivals, the minimum/maximum/median rates for different commodities on daily basis which will be stored on a server in Warana and will be accessible from any village booth in

Warana. This information is made available to all villagers in Marathi through the village booths. This system intends to bring complete agricultural marketing information at the door-steps of agriculturists in Warana.

Agricultural Schemes and Crop Technology

Nearly 80 per cent of the population of the Maharashtra state is directly or indirectly dependent on agriculture. The state government is implementing several schemes for the overall development of the farmers as well as for increasing their income. Through this system, the villagers can get a variety of information in the local language on agricultural schemes and crop technology such as new techniques, improved implements, new crop varieties, integrated pest management, etc.

Computer-based Self-Learning Aid

This application is designed as a 'Computer-based Self-Learning Aid' on topics such as Computer Science, English (grammar and vocabulary), History, Geography, General Awareness, Test of Reasoning, or any other subject where meaningful multiple choice quizzes can be set up.

It is menu driven and easy to operate. It provides an environment for self-learning through quizzes and inculcates the ability to administer a self-test after learning a lesson. The system permits the user to learn at his/her own pace and at a time convenient to him.

Village Information System

This system provides the user with the details about the amenities and other facilities that are available at his/her village or nearby villages such as the transport facilities (bus/railway), medical facilities, health services, postal services, banks, cooperative departments/stores. All this is available at the press of a button in the local language in the Village Information Booths.

Educational and Vocational Guidance

The educational and vocational guidance centres are located in the regional offices of the Maharashtra State Council of Educational Research and Training (MSCERT). They provide information to the students regarding different courses and careers through monographs. This information is now made available on the Internet. In the manual system, booklets and monographs are printed on various types of courses and careers and given to students visiting the centre. Each monograph contains a whole lot of information covering all the branches of chosen area, whereas a student needs the information pertaining to only one or two branches in which he is interested. Also, updation of monograph is not frequent. This new system will provide the latest information from any node of the network without actually visiting the centre and it is possible to give printouts of only those details which are required and of direct interest to the students, thus saving their valuable time.

Procedural Information System

The common man needs various types of government certificates and licenses like ration card, kerosene/gas licences, etc. Instead of approaching a number of different desks for getting them, this system facilitates the user to submit the requests at a 'single window', i.e., at one counter from where it is processed internally. It enables the user to save precious time and efforts and to overcome cumbersome processes. Further, the villager can obtain the application form and a list of the documents that are to be submitted along with the application.

Computerization of Warana Bazaar

Warana Grahak Mandal (Warana Bazaar) is the largest bazaar in Warana with the annual turnover of Rs 31 crore. It has an inventory of over 40,000 items. The items are not only sold at the Bazaar but are also sent to 29 outlets. Keeping track of this large inventory manually is a cumbersome process. This application aims to maintain the inventory through the bar code technology. The bar code technology ensures error free data entry using a hand-held bar code scanner. The application is expected to prove very beneficial to the management of Warana Bazaar in keeping track of the goods.

Wired Management of Sugarcane Cultivation

Sugar factory is the first and the largest cooperative business institution of the Warana complex. The sugarcane cultivators require information from the sugar factory for planning their schedules for sugarcane harvesting. The objective of this system is to facilitate the information entry at the village level and to automate sending and receiving of information and instructions from the sugar factory administration to the sugarcane growers in the village and vice versa. This would be effectively achieved by computerizing the entire information and using the computer network of 'Wired Village Project'.

Land Records Computerization (LRC)

This main objective of this project is to provide 7/12 extracts using the data on compact discs (CDs) at the village booths. The system also generates data from the village forms which provide details of ownership and crops. It further accepts additional data to generate eight different village forms. More transparency in land ownership and transactions can thus be achieved by the state government and the concerned officials which can go a long way in ensuring efficient administration.

Grievance Registration and Redressal System

This system enables the users to register their grievances and check the status of redressal. The grievance registration module uses the concept of Multiple Identity Number (MIN) to register the grievances. This MIN uniquely identifies the villager. The concept of MIN card has been used in the country for the first time.

The heart of the WWV project is its intranet. The intranet-based systems are the wired management of sugarcane cultivation, land records computerization, the computerization of the Warana Milk Dairy, and a Grievance Registration and Redressal System.

The content was created in the local Marathi language by the NIC office in Pune, Maharashtra State, through extensive interactions with the cooperatives. The content is regularly maintained and enhanced at the location of the central system within the local university. Among the web-based applications, the most extensively used are the procedural information system and the computerization of the Warana bazaar. This has relieved the villagers of cumbersome processes and long waits at government offices for certificates and licences such as ration cards and kerosene/gas licences.

Comments

The first phase of the Warana project has been completed successfully. The foundation has been laid and it is up to the Warana Cooperative Society to sustain the project.

Though application content is administered from the central hub, maintenance of the system is done in association with NIC, Pune. Again, like Gyandoot, the chief setbacks are due to connectivity and power fluctuations. All information technology centres are equipped with UPS; however, power is not guaranteed over a substantial period of time. Connections to the various nodes are maintained by a high-speed wireless LAN. The connections to the Internet however, were not of very high speed. This may be attributed to weather conditions on certain days.

The applications related to agriculture produce, schemes, and crop technology as well as for education are not being used to the fullest extent. One reason is the slow access to the Internet, insufficient awareness creation among the villagers, and the low levels of literacy in the area in spite of the high levels of income.

Similarly, the intranet-based applications that are extensively used are the wired management of the sugarcane cultivation and the computerization of the milk dairy as these relate directly to the economic lives of the villagers. While sugarcane cultivation is the main occupation of the farmers, milk production forms their secondary source of income. The impacts of both web-based and intranet-based systems on the villagers' lives are significant in their enhancement of the efficiency of the local economy and governance.

As in the Gyandoot project, there is a high dependence on the kiosk manager, due to low literacy among the farmers. Levels of trust between villagers and the kiosk managers are high due to the strength of the cooperative movement and the checks and controls it provides. As the kiosk manager works only part time and is paid a fixed salary, there is no incentive for him or her to maximize the use of the system. Moreover, as there are no charges for these services, it is difficult to expand the system, as there is dependence on external capital. All kiosk managers are male and usage of the system by women is low, as there is little information that is specially created for women users.

In order to improve the system further there is a need for:

(a) creation of a viable financial mechanism to convert this system into a pay-and-use one, to ensure its sustainability and expansion;
(b) encouragement of local villagers in additional content creation in general and specifically for women; and
(c) increasing the use of the system to maximize gains from the investment made. Kiosk managers need to be given incentives to increase the uses of the system to encourage literacy in the area as well as create a system whereby feedback from the users reaches the content creators and those who manage the system on a regular basis.

E-governance Project in Tamil Nadu

The Tamil Nadu government has adopted a strategy for designing and implementation of activities relating to governance of the state using the power of information technology. The e-governance strategy is in terms of specific governmental functions, viz., establishment of computer facilities and associated softwares at all taluk headquarters numbering 206 in the state and delivery of the services such as land records, old age pension, grievance petitions, issue of certificates and licence monitoring.

Sustainable Access in Rural India (SARI) Project

It is one of the several e-governance projects in Tamil Nadu. But this project has evoked more interest among researchers due involvement of several partners. The Sustainable Access in Rural India (SARI) project seeks to show that viable markets exist for information and communication services in rural poor areas by inventing and deploying innovative technologies, assessments, and business models. The ultimate goal is to link these activities to sustainable human development objectives.

SARI is part of the Digital Nations consortium of the MIT Media Lab and Harvard's Centre for International Development in collaboration with IIT, Chennai and the I-Gyan Foundation. Through the development and introduction of appropriate and enabling technologies and applications, SARI is expected to foster economic development and improve health and learning. It will have to do so in a financially sustainable way, even as it reaches into the poorest and most disadvantaged communities. SARI's diverse partnership of universities, non-profit and the private sector has begun to implement a unique project that will begin by wiring approximately one thousand neighbouring rural villages in each of two districts in the state.

SARI's magnitude is high because of large number of users, which helps and supports financial viability by aggregating demand, develops richer content and community by integrating people, and provides a powerful environment for research. There has been a great deal of enthusiasm about the value of information and communication technology (ICT) in the rural area of Tamil Nadu. The SARI project counts on its collaborative and interactive research agenda. The key research areas include: (1) technology, applications and content, (2) assessing social and economic impacts, and (3) business models for financially viable and self-sustaining access.

Highlights of SARI

- It uses a shared platform to deliver a variety of high quality services, allowing Internet access to be financially self-sustaining or profitable while reaching the rural poor.
- It helps markets to work by wiring regions densely and creating a local network effect. Putting at least one connection in each village will promote local/regional communication and information flows, while aggregating rural markets and attracting private sector interest.
- It creates and develops new access devices and applications to appropriately serve user needs and account for environmental conditions.
- It undertakes rigorous, non-anecdotal research on SARI's effects and the existence of rural information and communications markets.
- It offers access to schools and health clinics at low or no cost, and helps them learn to use it effectively.
- It values local champions and entrepreneurs and encourage their leadership; cooperate with residents and existing organizations.

It is held that SARI has been working successfully in 50 villages in northern Madurai district of Tamil Nadu state. Initial research activities included gathering data from households, NGO's, schools, health clinics and markets, on topics such as information needs, current communications options, socio-economic characteristics, and market activities. This information provided important market research for the design of locally relevant applications and content. The data was used to create relevant performance indicators (market and economic activities, functioning and performance of health clinics and schools) as a baseline against which to measure social and economic gains. There is also a significant research exploration on the technology of access, around issues such as cost, power, and appropriateness for environmental conditions. The Dhan Foundation (an NGO in South India) is assisting in various aspects of the start-up phase, and numerous other Indian organizations have volunteered their assistance as well.

The early applications and content includes an online spot labour market, market prices and other agricultural information, e-mail and voice messaging, and access to online government forms. There will be on-going evaluations conducted at three-month intervals. The primary purpose of the evaluations is to assess delivery and financial viability of services and impacts on social and economic development. These regular surveys provide important feedback into the design of more relevant content, applications and access devices.

As the project was successfully piloted in Madurai district, now it has been extended to nine more districts, viz., Cuddalore, Coimbatore, Kanchipuram, Theni, Thiruvallur, Nagapattinam, Tirunelveli, Salem and Erode. A total of Rs 30 crore has been spent for the project. It involves coordination among various players: government bodies, N-Logue, the implementing agency, local service providers who would set up access centres, and kiosk operators. The kiosks would help rural population in accessing the government offices at a fraction of cost and time.

Comments

While Tamil Nadu has made all the government forms available on the net without necessarily going into complicated ICT models, the real cake is taken by an entirely private agency, N-Logue, which has worked wonders in Madurai district. Using the wireless local loop technology and the available of optic fibre lines running across most of the districts, it made it profitable for private entrepreneurs to offer services, including that of e-governance, at the same time making a big difference to the lives of the rural citizens.

Success of this project is due to adoption of technology, as well as roping in with partners who offered services in the area of health, education, agriculture and, of course, the government that has been a major feature of the SARI. However, the government should think of more flexible and proactive methods of partnering with vendors if they have to get their projects implemented on time.

In short, a model for success that seems to work depends on political will, bureaucratic commitment and leadership in projects. With these in place, appropriate organization structure and required business processes will also emerge to fulfil the set objectives in the e-governance projects.

7

Issues and Challenges in the Information Technology Industry and Suggestions for Policy Implication

In this chapter, an analysis of various problems and challenges faced by this industry are outlined and suggestions are offered for improvement of the IT sector. General problems faced by this industry at the national level are discussed first, followed by specific problems of selected states.

General Problems of the IT Sector in India

India's Bandwidth Poverty

One of the major bottlenecks India is facing, is scarcity of bandwidth, specially when there has been no substantial increase in the international bandwidth availability. The higher growth rate for bandwidth requirement is due to the growing share of broadband access services in the total market. With factors such as the introduction of broadband Internet access services such as direct subscriber link (DSL) and cable, the corporate move toward Internet platforms and the growth of IT-enabled services are expected to drive the demand for bandwidth requirement. In addition, traffic management will become a difficult task with an increase in overseas-hosted content for local usage, convergence with wireless technologies, and applications such as video-on-demand, voice-over IP (VoIP), conferencing, and other broadband services. As per the estimate of NASSCOM, if India fails to increase Internet bandwidth availability, it will lose out on $22.5 billion by 2005. Currently, 325 MB/sec of international bandwidth is available, although the country has a current need for five GB/sec of bandwidth. In fact, McKinsey and Company also identified a lack of adequate bandwidth – both domestic and international – as one of the key infrastructure bottlenecks that would hold back India's capabilities to emerge as an IT superpower.

Bandwidth in India today is 180 times behind China, 400 times behind the United Kingdom, 500 times behind Japan, and 1,300 times behind the United States. Against India's mere 325 MB/sec, China, a late entrant, already has notched 55 GB/sec, the United Kingdom has 12 GB/sec, Japan has 160 GB/sec, and the United States has 500 GB/sec. Further, the United States is galloping toward vBNS (very high-speed Backbone Network Service), which is expected to achieve a few terabits per second (tbps).

Bandwidth is like roads – they are never enough. The higher the bandwidth is, the smoother the traffic. Bandwidth is the maximum amount of data that can be transmitted in a fixed amount of time. With more Indian companies using the IP (Internet Protocol) platform as an effective and secure medium for business transactions and communication, and with new-media firms offering services such as video-on-demand and media streaming, the demand for bandwidth is only going to shoot up. As India's Internet population increases exponentially in the coming years, the availability of bandwidth will be the key issue for the success of the information technology industry in the country.

Declining Profit Margin

In view of number of new players in the field, the competition is hotting up and raises the question: Will Indian IT industry achieve the vision of $50 billion target over a six-year period? The days of high margins are gone where they used to get 40-50 per cent margin. Now, IT industry is witnessing profit margins in the range of 13-15 per cent. Besides, the small and medium units are doing better in the field, forcing the large IT units to trim their waist. Further, the appreciation of rupee against US $ in recent days has affected operating margins of the IT exports.

Labour Attrition

It is well known the world over that India's main competitive advantage in software and services is its abundant, high quality and cost effective pool of skilled knowledge workers. Today, India is a magnet for software clients because of its vast resource of skilled manpower. The most immediate concern facing the industry is the increasing levels of attrition. Call centres, for instance, have an attrition rate of 30-35 per cent. Other than the natural rate of the attrition, 'poaching of employees', 'burnout' and high stress environments are causing an increasing churn rate.

Managing attrition is becoming increasingly important, not only because knowledge professionals are the lifeline of a service-oriented industry, but also staffing costs are one of the largest expenses regularly charged to the budget of a company in the IT/ITeS sector. When one counts salaries, benefits, bonuses, training and other personnel costs, companies invest a great deal of resources in their employees. Thus, attrition becomes a two-fold issue, one that is cost related and the second, retaining much needed and often, experienced talent. The challenge when addressing and understanding attrition, is that it involves people and is therefore tenuous and ridden with nuances. Therefore, the reason behind the high turnover rate cannot be reduced to a single factor, but instead a combination of workplace environmental influences and personal choices that people make.

Competition from China

Even as Indian IT industry's divine child – the software sector – trumpets its glorious achievements, its neglected step sibling – the hardware sector – is howling hoarse that their software kin better beware having built castles without a hardware base. China has 454 scientists and R&D personnel per million of population while India merely 149.

In terms of infrastructure, China has 125 million telephone lines compared to India's 30 million, 70 million mobile phones to India's 2.5 million, 22 million Internet subscribers to India's 1.5 million. By 2004, it will be 51 million Internet users in China compared to India's 15 million Internet users.

With A to Z of blooming and blossoming list of Silicon Valleys Changchun, Dalian, Guanghzhou, Hangzhou, Hefei, Shaanxi, Shenzhen, Xiqinghe, Wuhan, Zhongguanchun, IC Valley at Pudong, Free Trade Zone at Waigaoqiao, Notebook Valley in Kushan, Special Economic Zones in Shanzen, Shanton, Zhwhai, Liamen and Haimen, free ports and bonded zones at Dalian, Tianjin, Shanghai, Gimgzhow and Haimen, China is well on its way to become an IT superpower.

Having acquired competence in high-end IT design and manufacturing it is effectively leveraging upon this infrastructure intensive hardware base as a springboard to focus aggressively on software side of the industry, and predicted to become third largest semiconductor market in the world in three years. It is talking of IC Valleys and Notebook Zone and set to surpass US and host world's largest mobile telecommunication network. While its international bandwidth is already 1.2 gbps, whereas India with just 860 mbps pales in comparison. With sound hardware base China has enough muscle to go full steam ahead in software adding; huge domestic demand and ability to export have made it the preferred destination for investors.

Plagued by rampant piracy and being incapable of any software engineering, let alone technological innovations, China faces a plethora of problems with most enterprises looking for short-term gains and quick results, lack of strong computer industry for support, and missing the golden period of mid-80s while others concentrated on software, building itself up selling component and personal computers. Thus, software industry, without capital accumulation from hardware industry, is viewed as a child weaned of milk even since it was born and pins its hope on capital accumulation with people using software with copyright.

According to Yang, China will try to cultivate several powerful software bases as well as group of big software companies with annual output value of over 1 billion Yuan ($ 120 million) each in five to 10 years and expects its software export volume to increase to $1 billion by then, from current $130 million. She hopes to wield the baton to combat piracy to restore industry's health.

Indeed, it is yin and yang situation for both. But, does this mean India should take it easy. No, chorus industry watchers and experts. Observing China's ascendancy in software and R&D needs to be taken seriously, experts opined that the competition is good for Indian IT industry to move up the value chain and create strong differentiation for Indian R&D. Further, they note that India should focus on relentless R&D innovation to create technologies and products of superior value for worldwide adoption.

The threat is real. China may overtake India; it is possible that some Indian software MNCs may follow the so-called Ajantha clock route – if you can't beat China, join forces. In fact, some like Infosys already are on to this path. The big issue is China's hardware capability. Many big names already manufacture and some have engineering centres there. So, why should not the software be not developed in China?

Service Tax Issue

Since the service sector in the Indian economy is contributing 52 per cent to total GDP, the Government of India has announced recently the service tax to many areas in service sector including the IT sector. The service tax issue is one that continues to remain on the radar screens of the IT software and services sector, particularly the export segment within the industry. The government, in an attempt to boost the growth of software exporting companies, recently announced changes in the policies governing sales tax. It was decided for instance, that export of services would be exempt from this tax. While the government's initiative was positive and greatly welcomed by the industry, there were certain areas where tax is imposed. For instance, there is service tax on 'Business Auxiliary Service' of information technology industry payroll processing, accounts management, etc., even by using computer programs, would not be termed as activities primarily in relation to computer systems. The use of the computer in these services is secondary, while the primary activity is of business related work. Hence, these services would be taxable as Business Auxiliary Services.

However, IT services that were excluded from Business Auxiliary Service were services related to designing, developing or maintaining of computer software, computerized data processing, system networking and any other service involving the use of computer systems. The mere fact that a personal computer or a laptop was used for providing the service, did not, ipso facto, make the service an information technology service. Similarly, IT services have been used by the service provider, as input services would not automatically make the output services IT services. Any service of back office processing, primarily in relation to the operation of a computer system, would be covered as IT services, are not taxable. With regards to maintenance and repair services, the government has notified that such services would be exempt from service tax.

What is strange is that certain domestic IT-enabled services (ITeS) like payroll processing, accounts management will attract a sales tax of 8 per cent but the export of ITeS are exempted from this tax.

Obstacles for Growth of Domestic IT

There are, clearly, some constraints that are inhibiting the greater use of IT within India. Some of them are:

(i) *Lack of serious competition in most sectors*: Experience indicates that when there is competition, the pressure to improve efficiency and service necessitates the use of IT, making it a major strategic advantage. Indian examples of this include the banking and telecom sectors: both highly competitive and both big users of IT. Not surprisingly, there is a vast improvement in customer service in these sectors. The telecom sector has now become amongst the world's fastest growing and most efficient – the capital cost per line and the usage charges are amongst the world's lowest. Competition has led to substantial use of IT, and this has contributed to efficiency. However, this is not true with other service sectors of the economy.

(ii) *High cost of IT hardware in India*: Another inhabiting factor for slow growth of domestic IT is primarily due to high taxes and levies, including customs duties. It is estimated that these are at least two to three times higher than those elsewhere. This affects everything from individual ownership of PCs to corporate investments in IT infrastructure. One result is that computer penetration in India is less than one-fourth of that in China.

(iii) *The software industry has been very export focussed*: This seems to be an important cause of slow growth of the domestic market. While this observation has some merit, it is only partially true. Many software companies, especially small and medium enterprises, have actively pursued domestic opportunities. Some have created software specially for Indian companies, and a few have developed Indian language packages. However, more programmes appropriate for local companies, especially Small and Medium Enterprises (SMEs), and a greater thrust on Indian languages, can undoubtedly help stimulate demand. Indian information technology sector is dominated by only exports of services and honouring foreign clients. It is totally neglected in the development of information technology in domestic sector. There is a need for what is called "walking on two legs" (Schware, 1992). It is said that countries should target production and use in tandem, focusing on the interaction between production and use simultaneously.

(iv) *Government spending on IT has been small*: This has been an important constraining factor on market growth. Also, the spending has been skewed towards investments in hardware, at the cost of applications and services. The result has generally been poor return on investment, with few benefits. There have, of course, been some successes and a few states have taken noteworthy initiatives in the fields like e-governance, but these have been limited and the scaling-up has been slow. The Centre's efforts have yet been small and piece-meal. A large, imaginative programme could make a huge difference, not only for the IT industry, but also in terms of efficient, citizen-friendly and transparent governance.

(v) *Policy and regulatory bottlenecks are often important inhibitors to growth*: One example is the bar on using international call centre telecom equipment for domestic services. Permission to share the equipment will enable incremental pricing – and hence low cost – for domestic call centres; it will also bring international quality standards to the domestic market. A 'big bang' initiative could transform the scene: for example, zero taxes and duties on any PC of given specifications, which retails for less than say Rs 10,000. Such a challenge would benefit consumers and industry, while increasing overall efficiency through computer usage. A later nominal tax, once demand ramps up, would compensate for any short-term revenue loss to the government. Thailand is an example of bold initiatives to successfully increase PC penetration.

Slow Diffusion Challenges

Since skilled labour market is concentrated in South India and advance in technology is associated with an increase in the demand for skills, there is a slow diffusion of information technology to other states. It has become a big challenge to them especially northeastern part of India. No doubt, out of 28 states in India, nearly 18 states have announced their information technology policy by 2000, yet the penetration of information technology in such states is very slow; thus, it is a big challenge for equitable development of states.

Too Much Dependency on USA Market

As on 2001-02, out of total software exports of Rs 36,500 crore, almost 63 per cent was to Americas (USA, Canada and Latin America), 26 per cent to Europe, 24 per cent to Japan, and 27 per cent to rest of the world. Thus, USA continues to be India's largest export destination. This lead to a dependence syndrome. We have already faced a big challenge when terrorist attack on World Trade Centre in USA on September 11th affected US economy; in turn, Indian exports and personnel had to face a hard hit. Thus, there is a need for changing the direction of IT exports market destinations.

Difficulty in Moving Up the Value Chain

The moving up the value chain may not be a matter of pure choice but structurally limited. While there have been instance of Indian companies delivering high-end products (e.g., *BankAway* from Infosys for banking and e-commerce) the industry generally accepts that much of the exports from India consists of low-end outsourcing and IT-enabled services. This is due to barriers to entry into higher-end software.

Worsening the Existing Digital Divide

Given the current trends in industry, even on the software front the promise of information communication technology contributing to a redressal of national inequalities in technology and income is unlikely to be realized. This seems to be adding and even worsening the existing divide. The present study clearly reveals that the states which are lagging behind in adapting IT will have to go with high inequality and high computer illiteracy.

Neglect of Small and Medium Enterprises (SMEs) by STPs in India

The role of software technology parks in developing information technology sector is tremendous. Nearly 80 per cent of exports emanates from the units registered at STPs but most of them are large units. There is a hurdle of minimum export obligation of US $ 0.25 or three times of CIF value of imported capital goods, which ever is higher and the net foreign exchange earning of 10 per cent. This condition is not encouraging to SMEs in the industry. Considering the new emergent role of SME in recent years, there is a need to strengthen them.

Specific Problems of Selected States

Karnataka

Though Bangalore has got a range of IT-enabled service companies, it seems to be stronger in the call/contact centre, transcription, and back-office operations services. However, perhaps because of its information technology orientation, the city has also been able to attract a reasonable number of companies into database management/development, data processing/management and engineering design, and Geographical Information System (GIS) services. Given this, the city should still be able to attract other forms of IT-enabled service companies. However, some of the issues that need to be looked into are:

- The city's infrastructure, especially power and telecom, are not keeping pace with the information technology expansion. While the government promises uninterrupted power supply, the reality is far removed, and many IT-enabled service firms have to maintain their own back-up systems. This cranks up costs. In the early years of 1990s, information technology sector in the state has enjoyed the concession and tariffs on par with industry. But, recently, in the state of Karnataka, the information technology units are treated on par with commercial units and have to pay tariff at commercial rate. Besides, power-cut is a common phenomenon in this state due to shortage of power. This will affect those units totally dependent on Karnataka Power Transmission Corporation Limited (KPTCL).
- The city's public transport infrastructure is very weak and this has resulted in many people buying their own vehicle.
- While real estate is not a problem, property costs in Bangalore are higher than those in Chennai.

From the field study of Bhoomi e-governance project in Karnataka with a sample of 100 farmers, it is observed that the welfare gain accrued to the farmers due to computerized RTC is more than the welfare loss. Gain is in terms of reduction in level of harassment from the revenue officials and corruption. Besides, there is a large gain to the individual in terms of time saved from five days to one day in obtaining RTC through computer.

However, the welfare loss is also observed:

(1) In case of getting the mutation certificate from the officials (whenever there is need for transfer of ownership from parent/seller to child/purchaser) still officials have to be bribed.

(2) Though there is a 'good feel factor' to the majority of the farmers in getting the RTC without any harassment but in

monetary terms there is some loss to them. Since most of the kiosks are at taluk (sub-district level) every farmer has to travel from his village to the taluk office. He has to incur not only travel cost but also other incidental expenses toward tea, meals, etc., and also has to loose one day wage/work during his visit. Therefore, almost all (100) respondents felt that the kiosk should be at the Hobli or panchayat level.

(3) Since the computer operators are working as part-time workers on consolidated salary of Rs 2,000–3,000, sometimes they play truant on the excuse of technical deficiency or lack of electricity or something else. Some of the respondents expressed that extra money is demanded by the operators for urgent issue of RTC.

(4) Since the farmers are illiterate, they do not remember the survey number of their own piece of land. Again they have to approach village accountant and get the number. Only after providing survey number and paying fee of Rs 15, the farmer gets a computerized RTC. Thus, illiteracy among farmers many a times takes a way the possible gain from the kiosk. This illiteracy and ignorance give scope to the middleman; therefore, there are still mediators exploiting the farmers in the system.

(5) The installation of touch-screen facility in one or two revenue divisions and its use is not frequently done by farmers. It does not serve the purpose, except that they can just view the RTC on the computer. Hence, authorities should try to replace it by a scanning machine. Scanning machine may be helpful in processing of application at the time of issue of mutation certificate.

Andhra Pradesh

The experience of IT-led growth has shown an overemphasis on urban areas and certain regions to the absence of a more equitable regional development. There are apprehensions that the information technology-led economic growth may contribute to widening of rural urban disparities, as the evidence shows both within and outside.

The service sector contributes about 45 per cent of the State domestic product in Andhra Pradesh. About 73 per cent of population in the state lives in rural areas characterized by low productivity. This is reflected in the low share of primary sector (26%). Strengthening of urban sector is imperative for increasing the share of tertiary activities. It is however, also argued that the vision of India as a knowledge based economy can be realized only when it is based on the foundation of a robust industrial economy.

The basic challenges lie in improving the social sectors like education, health, poverty, etc., and developing infrastructure. If these problems are not tackled on a priority basis, the fast-growing information technology sector will leave majority of the population behind that may lead to a more iniquitous and polarized society. Thus, there is a need for a greater thrust in the policy framework in Andhra Pradesh towards making information technology an enabler and equalizer in opportunities and development. The information technology e-governance projects depend on trickle down effects of information and communication technology, which have no direct attack on enhancing agriculture production and productivity, which would have an immediate impact on poverty.

Tamil Nadu

Chennai, despite a relatively sturdy infrastructure, has not been able to attract as many information technology enabled service firms as Bangalore. However, from the profile of the companies operating in the city, it seems that the city is strong in call/contact centre, content management/development and animation, data processing, management, digitization, website services and web applications. The city has the potential to attract all types of IT-enabled service firms, provided it addresses the following issues:

- Chennai loses out to the likes of Delhi and Bangalore in the perception game. The city is perceived to be conservative and lacking in infrastructure. It would help if the government found a way to highlight the success stories of companies based in Chennai.
- The lack of neutral English accent among the local populace is a problem that needs to be addressed.

Maharashtra

Mumbai

Mumbai is strong in call/contact centres, back-office operations, and data processing/management. However, it seems to be quite weak in transcription services and network management/maintenance. There is a problem of high dependence on the kiosks managers of WWV project in Maharashtra, due to low literacy among the farmers and slow access to Internet, as the managers work only part-time and is paid a fixed salary. There is no incentive for him to maximize the use of the system. There are no charges for the services in such kiosks in Maharashtra. It is difficult to expose the system and sustain over a long period. The city holds the potential to attract all kinds of IT-enabled service companies, but at the same time, it needs to take some steps maintain and improve its competitiveness. These are:

- Mumbai is plagued by high real estate rates. Even a depressed real estate market has failed to bring down the prices on par with the other metros.
- Though Mumbai has adequate trained manpower, the cost is among the highest in the country.
- Though Mumbai has the best public transport infrastructure in the country, the same cannot be said about its road network. The city's congested roads need to be de-clogged.

Pune

Though Pune has not managed to attract many IT-enabled service companies, those that are there, seem to be evenly distributed between the call/contact centre, data processing/ management/digitization and back-office business. But, the other services are conspicuous by their absence. Infrastructure tops the list of concerns. A reliable and continuous power supply needs to be provided. Currently, IT-enabled service companies need to have their own back-up power system to supplement the utility's supply. Some of the other concerns are:

- A rickety public transport system forces firms to spend on transportation. Additionally, the road network needs to be expanded on a fast track.
- Despite the government's sops for IT-enabled service units real estate rates in Pune are not that low.

Suggestions to General Problems

In this section, suggestions are offered for policy purpose. The suggestions are merely indicative of the direction in which the action is needed. Social science research always tends to suggest a tentative measures for the improvement of the situation. In the light of this, some suggestions are offered under general and specific categories to the respective problems.

(1) The per capita bandwidth squeeze in India stems from three basic constraints: access lines, weak PSTN (Public Switched Telephone Network) based national backbone, and a bottleneck to international gateways. If private firms are allowed to lease bandwidth from these undersea cables, the bandwidth problem could be addressed to a large extent. VSNL, however, has declared that it would add another 185 MB/sec international bandwidth in a couple of months to tackle the increasing bandwidth requirements in the country.

Government should allow IT-enabled services to have their own international gateways. Quality bandwidth is essential for IT-enabled services such as call centres and medical transcription, considering that India has such major stakes in web-enabled services, which is expected to grow to a $10 billion industry very soon, the government should allow them to have their bandwidth. Apart from the IT-enabled services industry, some other segments that would require increased Internet bandwidth are business to business and business to consumer, communication entertainment, residential video services, and education. It is high time the government decentralized and decontrolled bandwidth allocation. Experts predict that Internet connections in India will exceed the 10 million mark within three years. In addition, dramatic growth in India's software industry, the rise in cable TV are expected to contribute to the country's bandwidth dilemma. But private investors, along with the government, are working to solve India's bandwidth problem.

Private sector leaders and state run giants have lined up investment totaling at least $5 billion to build domestic fibre optic pipes that will carry sound, pictures, and text. From state-owned power utilities to telecom to multi-business corporations, everybody is keen on wiring India. Perhaps, all of these initiatives combined will help to solve India's growing bandwidth dilemma. But without a doubt, it will take years, and it is hoped that these investors both private and public will be able to keep up the pace with the demands of the Internet, its related technology, and its insatiable army of users.

(2) If our vision is to be software powerhouse, hardware industry needs to be resilient and vibrant. The constraints one sees in this direction are in infrastructure and decentralized decision-making processes. We have not been able to have minimum 4 per cent sales tax goal achieved for IT hardware. But this is typical for IT hardware. Infrastructure is not just telecom and bandwidth, it is airports, roads, power and well-planned townships, that help market Indian software as a brand. In fact, it is easier as it is

acknowledged that Indians produce good software. What is needed is both.

(3) Rural India is potentially, a big market. Apart from projects for citizen-services in several States, examples like ITC's e-choupal indicate the feasibility and financial viability of e-procurement and e-commerce in the agricultural arena. This is now being extended to things like selling insurance policies, FMCG items, etc. Gyandoot in MP provides horoscope and matrimonial services. Clearly, we are yet only scratching the surface of what is certainly a massive market. Importantly, growth in the domestic market will also help the IT hardware industry. Greater IT usage in the country will also have other spin-off benefits. It is established that IT, by bringing in transparency, reduces corruption. Karnataka's computerized land-records project, Bhoomi is an example of this. IT also helps to catalyse a new work culture, with emphasis on quality and care for detail.

(4) Removing the unnecessary obstacles and putting in place positive policies, will help to boost the domestic market. The government, IT industry and users each need to take responsibility. A private-public partnership between the government and industry, as in software exports, could double growth rates, with big economic and societal benefits.

(5) NASSCOM feels that identification of a defensible niche is the first step for a small company to differentiate. In terms of verticals, SME players could target emerging or nascent verticals such as transportation, education, utilities and e-governance. In terms of technology, there are several niche technology areas such as embedded systems, Geographical Information System (GIS) and web services. SME players could also look at playing a big role in the products or components segment. Though a high-risk space, a product play is more suitable for a small player as it is comparatively scale independent. Companies could

aim to start with components as opposed to full fledged product suites. NASSCOM has proposed some initiatives for this segment including:

- Helping SMEs in spotting opportunities by a market intelligence service through identification of new business areas and technologies – this information will be mailed to SMEs on a weekly basis.
- Holding niche events in verticals and geographies for SMEs.
- Public Relation effort for SME companies.
- Helping SME companies understand best practices by holding workshops on quality, salary and people practices.

(6) In the backdrop of intense competition and falling billing rates, the high rate of attrition is set to pose a major threat to the fast-growing IT-enabled services (ITeS)/business process outsourcing (BPO) industry. With attrition levels hovering between 30 per cent and 35 per cent, attrition is fast becoming a much-talked about problem in the ITeS/BPO sector. The most immediate need is to address the issues of high attrition level in this industry by identifying the drivers.

Though India boasts of a large, highly-skilled talent pool, one of the major challenges it faces is making sure that this talent pool is sustainable in the long run. Developing new talent is a long-term imperative, however, the need of the hour is to arrest the growing attrition rate.

Some of the major drivers of a high attrition rate are workplace environmental influences and personal choices that people make. Issues such as vague vision and values, lack of positive direction, mixed messages, limited or lack lustre training, wrong hiring, mismatched measures and rewards, overworked employees and burnout are behind the increasing attrition rates.

Therefore, the ITeS industry should invest in their employees in the form of salaries, benefits, bonuses, training and other personal costs. The needs of employees have to be balanced with that of the customers and the business, it added. This is where the art of balancing and making trade-offs come into play.

Like most customers, employees are reasonable and willing to focus on the greater good as long as they share in the success and rewards. It is important to remember that retaining productive employees results in higher customer satisfaction and lower costs.

(7) In order to sustain the growth of both output and employment in this sector, there is a need for strengthening the domestic hardware production and move up the value chain in software. This requires the state to play a more proactive role of influencing the pattern of growth rather than leave matters to the market.

(8) The state's role is more crucial when we examine the prospect of sharply widening digital divide within the economy. With literacy and schooling achievements still at indefensibly low level, the first task would be to rapidly advance in providing a minimum degree of access to information and communication technology to those who are completely disconnected. No democratic society can tolerate growing divisions of this kind, making effective state intervention in bridging the digital divide is an absolutely necessity.

(9) Since the industry is already 10-year-old there is no need for further concessions to this sector. However, there is a clear cut policy to remove the ambiguities. For instance certain domestic IT-enabled services like pay roll processing, accounting management attracted a sales tax of 8 per cent but at the same time export services are exempted from this tax. This kind of anomaly should be removed. A uniform 4 per cent sales tax on all kinds of IT services (domestic or export) is feasible from the point of sustainable development of this sector.

(10) Slow diffusion is a big threat to the balanced development of the economy. Regions which are ahead will surely surge further and those laggards lag behind. All the states have to announce their own IT policy and implement whole heartedly by making use of the technology for their domestic sector. The typical example is the state of Madhya Pradesh. Though this state is not counted much in the contribution of IT sector to SDP but IT use in rural economy through 'Gyandoot' is commendable. This is what the other states have to follow.

(11) Dependency syndrome on US economy needs reconsideration. It is not always feasible to put all eggs in one basket. Changing the direction of trade to other market, even with low profit margin can avoid the big risk of total dependency on big brother.

(12) SME sector is a major player and a strong SMEs' sector is critical to terms of services, that it can provide to the large and medium enterprises. In developed countries, large enterprises are depending on the network of SMEs, hence the technology strong SMEs system in India is essential to develop, attract and work with larger enterprises.

(13) China's ascendancy in software and R&D needs to be taken seriously. Unless India focus relentlessly on R&D innovation to create technologies needed for world wide adoption, it is difficult to retain the present position. In case, if it is too difficult to compete with China the only way is to join hands with her. Indian MNC, Infosys is already moving in this direction.

Suggestions to Specific Problems of Selected States

The specific problems of states identified earlier will have to be tackled by the following suggestions:

Karnataka

(1) There is a pertinent problem of power and roads that needs to be looked into on priority basis. Further, the welfare loss in obtaining RTC through computer is

observed in the field study. This loss pertained to travel cost from villages to taluk and incidental expenses towards tea, coffee, meals, etc., during their visit. In order to avoid this monetary loss, we suggest that kiosk should be established at Hobli or panchayat level.

(2) The computer operators in kiosk are working as part-time workers on consolidated salary basis. The operators should be given work on commission basis so that they will evince more interest in their work.

(3) The instalation of the touch-screen facility did not serve the purpose, hence authority should try to replace it by scanning machine which may be helpful in processing of application in the issue of mutation certificate. It will avoid the corruption at mutation level as the entry of sale deed and katha transfer application is made in the computer through scanning machine. Thus, total transparency is to be maintained.

Andhra Pradesh

The policy has urban bias and neglected the old economy industries and rural economy. There is a need for balanced policy approach.

Tamil Nadu

There is a conservative approach and neutral English accent among the local populace that needs to be addressed.

Maharashtra

The high cost of trained manpower and congested roads that are bothering and there is need for taking action to tackle these for sustainable development of information technology in all sectors of the economy.

Conclusion

In short, the sustainable development of information technology sector across the states in the country depends on the following:

(1) Emphasis on production of IT close to use and that build capabilities.
(2) Diffusion of IT to manufacturing and agriculture sectors.
(3) Strengthening the government investment in domestic sector.
(4) Enhancing the scope of software technology parks so as to include small and medium enterprises.
(5) The fast growth of information technology sector in leading state governments is partly due to exemption from taxes, concessions and rebate on land acquisition, relaxations in Acts as well as support service rendered by them. There is a lesson to other non-leading states to follow the suit.

This will go a long way in sustaining the development of IT sector and making a niche in the development of Indian economy.

Bibliography

Abramovitz, Moses and Paul A. David, (1999), *American Microeconomic Growth in the Era of Knowledge-Based Progress: The Long-Run Perspective,* Stanford Institute for Economic Policy Research, Discussion Paper Series, Stanford University, December.

Ahluwalia, Montek S. (2002), "State Level Performance under Economic Reforms in India", in A. Krueger, (ed.), *Economic Policy Reforms and the Indian Economy,* Chicago, University of Chicago Press.

Arora, A. and Arunachalam, V.S. (2000), "The Globalization of Software: The Case of the Indian Software Industry", A report submitted to the Sloan Foundation, Crnegie Mellon University, Pittsburgh PA. http:/www.Heinz.cmu.edu/project/India/publications.html

Arora, A., Arunachalam, V.S., Asundi, J. and Fernandes, R. (2001a), "The Indian Software Service Industry", *Research Policy,* Vol. 30, p. 1267-87.

Arora, A., Gambardella, A. and Torrisi, S. (2001b), "In the footsteps of the Silicon Valley? Indian and Irish Software in the International Division of Labour", paper presented at the conference, *Silicon Valley and Its Imitators,* Stanford Institute for Economic Policy Research, July 2000.

Bajpai and Dokeniya, A. (1999), "Information Technology-Led Growth Policies: A Case Study of Tamil Nadu", Development Discussion Paper no. 729, October, Harvard Institute for International Development.

Bajpai, (2000), "Rising Global Competitiveness of Tamil Nadu's IT Industry", *Economic and Political Weekly,* 35(6), p. 449-65.

Bala Subrahmanya M.H. (2004), *Industrial Economics: Indian Empiricism,* Wisdom House Publications Ltd., England, Ch. 10, p. 217-229.

Banerjee, A.V. and Duflo, E. (2000), "Reputation Effects and the Limits of Contracting: A Study of the Indian Software Industry", *Quarterly Journal of Economics,* Vol. 15(3), p. 989-1017.

Bhatnagar, S. and Schware, R. (2000), *Information and Communication Technology in Development: Cases from India.* New Delhi, Sage.

Bjorhus, J. (2002), "India's Infosys Struggles through Transformation", *San Jose Mercury News*, 11 February, p. 1E.

Brynjolfsson, E. and Yang, S. (1996), "Information Technology and Productivity: A Review of the Literature", *Advances in Computers* 43:179-214 and L. Hitt (1996), "Paradox lost? Firm-level evidence of high returns to information systems spending". *Management Science* 42: 541-58.

—, (2002), *Understanding the Digital Economy: Data, Tools and Research,* Cambridge, Massachusetts, MIT Press.

—, and Hitt (1995), "Information Technology as a Factor of Productivity: The Role of Differences among Firms", *Economics of Innovation and New Technology,* 3 (3-4): 183-99.

Business Week (2001), "India 3.0: Its Software Outfits Take On the World", 26 February, p. 44-46.

Carmel, E. (1995), "Entrepreneurial Technologists may have the upper hand in Global Software Competition", *Research-Technology Management*, 38: 10-1.

Dewan, S. and Kraemer, K.L. (1998), "International Dimensions of the Productivity Paradox", *Communication of the AGM*, 41 (8): 56-62.

David, Paul (2000), "Understanding Digital Technology's Evolution and the Path of Measured Productivity Growth: Present and Future in the Mirror of the Past", in Brynojolfsson and Kahin (2000).

Deccan Herald (2002), "IT Sector may achieve $50 billion exports by 2008", says Study, 11 June.

Dedrick, J. and Kraemer, K.L. (1998). *Asia's Computer Challenge: Threat or Opportunity for the United States and the World?* New York: Oxford University Press.

—, and Choi D.W. (1995), "Korean Industrial Policy at a Crossroad: The Case of Information Technology", *Journal of Asia Business*, 11 (4): 1-33.

—, Yamashiro (2000), "Refining and Extending the Business Model with Information Technology: Dell Computer Corporation", *The Information Society*, 16 (1): 5-21.

—, Goodman, S. and Kraemer, K.L. (1995), "Little Engines that Could: Computing in Small, Energetic Countirs", *Communications of the ACM*, 38 (5): 21-6.

DeLong, J.B. and Summers, L.H. (1991), "Equipment Investment and Economic Growth", *Quarterly Journal of Economics*, 106: 445-503.

Desai, R.G. (2001), "Changing Employment and Sectoral Contribution in India: Role of Information Technology", *Southern Economist*, Bangalore, 15 September.

—, (2003), "Information Technology and Growth at Regional Level: A Study of Leading States in India", *Productivity,* National Productivity Council, New Delhi, Vol. 44, No. 1, April-June, p. 55-62.

Desai, A.V. (2000), "The Peril and the Promise: Broader Implications of the Indian Presence in Information Technologies", Working Paper, August, CREDPR, Stanford University.

Dewan, S. and Kraemer, K.L. (2000), "Information Technology and Productivity: Evidence from Country-level Data", *Management Science*, 46: 548-62.

The Economist (2001b), "Outsourcing to India: Back Office to the World", 5 May, p. 59.

Eischen, K. (2000), "National Legacies, Software Technology Clusters and Institutional Innovation: The Dichotomy of Regional Development in Andhra Pradesh, India", University of California, Department of Sociology.

Gibbs, W.W. (1994), "Software's Chronic Crisis", *Scientific American*, 271(3), 86-95.

Gordon, Robert J. (1999), "Has the 'New Economy' Rendered the Productivity Slowdown Obsolete", available at http://faculty-We.at. Northwestern.edu/economics/Gordon/researchhome.html.

Government of India (1991), "India's New Industrial Policy: Tabled in both the Houses of Parliament", 24 July.

Government of India (2002), *"Information Technology: Annual Report"*, Ministry of Information Technology, New Delhi.

Greenwood, J. and Yorukoglu, M. (1997). "1974", Carnegie: Rochester Conference Series on Public Policy, 46: 49-95.

Grieco, J.M. (1984), *Between Dependency and Autonomy: India's Experience with the International Computer Industry*, Berkeley and Los Angeles, University of California Press.

Hanna, N. (1994), "Exploiting Information Technology for Development: A Case Study of India", World Bank, Discussion Paper no. 246.

Heeks, R. (1998), "The Uneven Profile of India's Software Exports", IDPM Working Paper No. 3, October, University of Manchester.

Heeks, R. (1996), *India's Software Industry: State Policy, Liberalization and Industrial Development,* New Delhi, Thousand Oaks and London, Sage.

Huge (1991), "Regional Formation of High-technology Services Industries: The Software Industry in Washington State", *Environment and Planning,* A, 23, 867-84.

India Today (2000), "Is E-governance for Real?". 11 December, p. 70-75.

Jagdish S. (2003), "The Ice has Broken with ICT", *Deccan Herald*, May, 12.

Jorgenson, D.W. and Stiroh, K. (1995), "Computers and Growth", *Economics of Innovations and New Technology*, 3: 295-316.

Joseph, K.J. (2002), "Growth of ICT and ICT for Development: Realities of Myths of Indian Experience", Discussion papers. No. 2002/78, Helsinkv-UNU/WIDER.

Kaushikm, P.D. and Singh, Nirvikar (2002), "Information Technology and Broad Based Development: Preliminary Lessons from North India", UC Santa Cruz Working Paper.

Kiran, Karnik (2003), NASSCOM FY 03: Software and Service Industry Performance, July 18.

Kraemer, K.L. and Dedrick, J. (1994), "Payoffs from Investment in Information Technology: Lessons from the Asia-Pacific Region". *World Development*, 22: 1921-31 (2001).

—, Lal, K. (2000a), "Adoption of Information Technology and its consequences in a Development Context: A Study of Indian Electrical and Electronic Goods and Garments Sectors in Two Industrial Clusters", Amsterdam, Thela Publishers.

—, (2001b), "Institutional Environment and Development of Information and Communication Technology in India", *The Information Society,* 17(2).

—, (1999c), "Information Technology and Exports: A Case Study of Indian Garments Manufacturing Enterprises", published as discussion paper (externally reviewed) No. 15, September, Centre for Development Research (ZEF), Bonn.

—, (2002d), "E-business and Manufacturing Sector: A Study of Small and Medium-sized Enterprises in India", *Research Policy* (North Holland).

Lehr, W. and Lichtenberg, F. (1999), "Information Technology and its Impact on Productivity: Firm Level Evidence from Government and Private Data Sources", *Canadian Journal of Economics*, 32: 335-62.

Loveman, G.W. (1998), "An Assessment of the Productivity Impact on Information Technologies", Working Paper No. 88-054, Cambridge, MIT Press.

Manu, N. Kulkarni (2003), "Beyond Computerization of Land Records", *Economic and Political Weekly,* June 14-20, 2003.

—, (2002), "Whither e-governance in Karnataka?, *Deccan Herald*, August 15.

Mansell, R. and Wehn, U. (1998) (eds.), *Knowledge Societies: Information Technology for Sustainable Development*, Oxford, Oxford University Press.

Matti, Pohjola (2001), (ed.), *Information Technology Productivity and Economic Growth*, New York, Oxford University Press.

Miller, Robert R. (2001), "Leapfrogging? India's Information Technology Industry and the Internet", IFC Discussion Paper No. 42, May, The World Bank, Washington DC.

Mody, A. and Dahlman, C. (1992), "Performance and Potential of Information Technology: An International Perspective", *World Development*, 20: 1703-19.

NASSCOM (2003), National Association of Software and Service Companies, Various Reports and Press Releases.

Negroponte, N. (1995), *Being Digital*, New York, Knopf. (1998). "The Third shall be the First", Wired 6.01.

Singh, Nirvikar (2003), "Information Technology as an Engine of Broad-Based Growth in India" in *The Knowledge Economy in India*, F.G. Richter and P. Banerjee (eds.), New York, Palgrave, Macmillan.

OECD (1998), "Use of Information and Communication Technology at Work". OECD, DSTI/ICCP/IE (97)8/FINAL.

Panagariya, A. (2001), "Abolish this Monopoly", *Economic Times*, 28 March.

Pant, K.C. (1999), "Certain Aspects of Technology and Economic Developments in India: Preparation of India for the New Millennium", address at the Kellogg School of Management, Chicago, U.S.A., 11, November.

Parente, S. (1994), "Technology Adoption, Learning-by-doing, and Economic Growth". *Journal of Economic Theory*, 63: 346-69.

Prahalad, C.K. and Hart, S.L. (2002), "The Fortune at the Bottom of the Pyramid", http://www.strategy-business.com/media/pdf/02106.pdf

Quah, Danny (2000), "Weightless Economy in Economic Development" in Matti Phojola, (ed.), *IT: Productivity and Economic Growth*, New York, Oxford Press, Ch. 4, p. 72.

Ramachandraiah, C. (2003), "Information Technology and Social Development", *Economic and Political Weekly*, March 22.

Rao, R.L.R. (1995), "Second Wave of Software Investment to Flow into Bangalore", *Economic Times*, 10 May.

Romer, P. (1993), "Ideas Gaps and Object Gaps in Economic Development", *Journal of Monetary Economics*, 32:543-73.

Ray, D. (1998), *Development Economics*, Princeton, Princeton University Press.

Reilly, K.T. (1995), "Human Capital and Information", *Journal of Human Resource*, 30: 1-18.

Sacenian, A. (2000), "The Bangalore Boom: From Brain Drain to Brain Circulation?", in K. Keniston and D. Kumar (eds.), *Bridging the Digital Divide: Lessons from India*, Bangalore, National Institute of Advanced Study.

Sacenian, A. (2001), "Bangalore: The Silicon Valley of Asia?", Working paper No. 91, Centre for Research on Economic Development and Policy Reform, Stanford University, February.

Schreyer, P. (1998), "Information and Communication Technology and The Measurement of Real Output, Final Demand and Productivity", OECD/STI Working Paper 1998/2.

Schware, R. (1992), "Software Industry entry Strategies for developing Countries: A 'walking on two legs' proposition", *World Development*, 20: 143-64.

—, and Carmel, E. (1995), "Entrepreneurial Technologies may have the Upper Hand in Global Software Competition: Research-Technology Management", 38: 10-1.

Sebastian, Morris, (2003), "Competition, Regulation and Strategy: The Information Technology Industry", *Economic and Political Weekly*, August 16.

SGKI (2000), Subject Group on Knowledge-based Industries, Prime Minister's Council on Trade and Industry, *Recommendations of the Task Force on Knowledge-based Industries*, Prime Minister's Office, New Delhi. http://www.nic.in/pmcouncils/reports/knowl/

Shaw, K. (1998), "By What means does Information Technology affect Employment and Wages" paper prepared for the conference on Information and Communication Technologies, Employment and Earnings, Nice, June.

Sichel, D.E. (1997). *The Computer Revolution: An Economic Perspective*, Washington DC: Brookings Institution Press.

Siegel, D. (1997), "The impact of Computers on Manufacturing Productivity Growth: A Multiple-indicators, Multiple-causes Approach". *The Review of Economics and Statistics*, 74:68-78.

Solow, R.M. (1957), "Technical Progress and the Aggregate Production Function" *Review of Economic and Statistics*, 39: 312-20.

—, (1987), "We'd Better Watch Out", New York, Review of Books, July-12.

Sruti, Changati (2003), "IT Act-Danger or Violation of Civil Rights", *Economic and Political Weekly.*

Subramanian, C.R. (1992), *India and the Computer: A Study of Planned Development*, New Delhi, Oxford University Press.

Tang, P., Powell, D. and Tunzelmann, N. von (1997), "The Development and Application of New Information Technology Development and Energy", European Parliament, March.

UNCSTD (1997). "Substantive Theme: Information and Communication Technologies for Development", *Report of the Working Group on* Information Technologies for Development.

UNCTAD (1993), "Information Technology and International Competitiveness: The Case of the Construction Service Industry", New York, United Nations.

UNDP (2001), "Making New Technologies Work for Human Development", Human Development Report, Oxford, Oxford University Press.

Vijay Kumar, R. (2002), "Bhoomi earns kudos for government", Southern States of Karnataka, *The Hindu*, December-17.

Woodall, P. (2000), "The New Economy", *The Economist*, September 23, Survey, p. 6.

www.digitaldividends.org

www.iee.org/Publish/INSPEC/

www.infosys.com

www.hcltechnologies.com

www.wipro.com

www.bea.org

www.redherring.com (Technology Trends)

www.cio.com

www.mckinseyquartely.com

www.inomics.com

www.fastcompany.com

www.jama.org

www.stpi.soft.net

www.nasscom.org

www.bangaloreit.com

www.rediff.com

www.stpmum.soft.net

www.gyandoot.net

www.iadb.org

www.revdpt.kar.nic.in

www.indiastat.com

www.ap-it.com

Index